Betty Salpekar

SOLEFULL SOCKS

Knitting from the Ground Up

Foreword by Cat Bordhi

Photography by Barbara Benson

Text and illustrations copyright © 2014 Betty Salpekar

Back cover: author photograph © 2014 Nick Salpekar
All other photographs copyright © 2014 Barbara Benson

Book Design: Zoë Lonergan
Photography: Barbara Benson
Editorial Consultant: Deborah Robson
Technical Editor: Jamie McCanless

First published in 2014 by
Bread Crumbs Press
PO Box 2423
Woodstock, GA 30188

www.solefullsocks.com

Printed and bound in China through Asia Pacific Offset

ISBN-13: 978-0-9897365-0-3

Library of Congress Control Number: 2013913843

10 9 8 7 6 5 4 3 2 1

To my father for showing me the joy of elegant innovation

To my husband for showing me the value of resolute perseverance

> "
>
> We create for the
> same reason we
> breathe — we need to.
>
> Rafe Esquith
>
> "

Table of Contents

Foreword

BY CAT BORDHI

Given time and perspective, most initial infatuations fade. On rare occasions, they endure and deepen. Betty's work, which I think of as ceremonial clothing for the foot, is of that rare and certain brilliance. I am reluctant to classify her Solefull masterpieces as mere socks, for they seem to be an entirely new class of footwear.

My head-over-heels infatuation with Solefull socks began in 2009 when I was a judge for the XRX Think Outside the Sox contest. During the long day of judging, again and again I returned to one sock in particular, an ornately carved cream sock titled "Budapest Roof Tiles Socks." Its impeccable workmanship, elegance, and architectural courage could have been the work of a Renaissance master. I actually wondered if it could have been taken from a museum collection. Several years previously, I had experimented with a visually similar architecture and reluctantly abandoned it because I couldn't master key structural and design issues. And now here I was, holding the fully realized form in my hands, all issues resolved, harmonized, and transcended by a mysterious person whom I clearly had to meet.

Another very different yet architecturally identical pair of socks, "Leopard Spot Socks", won the grand prize in spite of my arguments for the Budapest sock. It turned out that Betty had sent in both entries. At the awards banquet, my hero, who unlike many of the other winners, happened to actually be there, rose from the sea of knitters and made her way to the stage—such good fortune for both of us, it turned out. On stage, I think I whispered in Betty's ear that we had to talk. Later that night I extracted her from the crowd and informed her that she had to write a book on her architecture and that I and our Visionary Group, a fiercely intelligent community of knit designers dedicated to helping one another self-publish books of enduring and unique value, would welcome her at our next annual retreat and freely share knowledge and support.

I may have also mentioned that birthing a book would be a big job. Magnificent books take longer to complete than any author expects; Betty's has taken nearly 4 years, and the content has ripened, expanded, and been distilled into the powerful collection you now hold. In my opinion it is the very best book on knitted footwear in the world, ever. It soars beyond my lofty expectations, and I have a secret to share: There is more. Much more. When Betty laid out dozens of socks at her first Visionary Retreat, the consensus was that there was more than could fit in one book; in fact, there were at least two categories of the architecture. So even if it takes another four years, wait patiently for what comes next. Although I only get to see and hold (and try on!) Betty's socks once a year at our retreats, their beauty and vitality sing to me like a muse all year long. Betty's work is indeed of rare and certain brilliance, and with this book she has placed it in your hands in the most practical manner possible.

Introduction

WHY SOLEFULL?

It all started because of where holes used to appear in my hand-knitted socks. They were under the ball of the foot, sometimes under the heel. They never came at the back of the heel or on the toe, where it's easy to carry along reinforcement yarn when knitting socks either toe-up or top-down. Yes, I could mend those holes. But it seemed like there should be some way to prevent them, or at least delay them a lot. The quest to find that way took me on quite a journey, which I'll retrace for you below. In the course of it I came to discover what I call, borrowing from Cat Bordhi's idea of socks having an architecture, the *solefull sock architecture*. I call the structure *solefull* because you knit the sole in full as the first step in making the sock.

As we begin this solefull journey, I am delighted to report that the architecture I devised did far more than solve that original problem. The initial impetus was entirely practical, but the final solution offers unexpected aesthetic delights and an unusually comfortable fit. It opens up unique ways to create patterns within the sock form. I have spent years happily experimenting with this structure for reasons that have nothing to do with durability.

If you'd like a quick, visual rationale for learning to make socks this way, simply thumb through the photos of the designs presented in this book. Each idea that I experimented with led to many more. All of the patterns and ideas flow out of the architecture naturally. Once you understand the structure, you will find that it encourages creativity.

If you'd like a more abstract idea of why you might want to learn the solefull approach, here is a list of the benefits that come from knitting socks this way.

First, the **practical matters** relating to where I began—with the sole, and with reinforcing, replacing, or making it more comfortable. You can:

- *carry a reinforcement yarn on just the sole*
- *reinforce the entire sole*
- *re-sole a sock without disturbing the top*
- *cushion the sole by knitting it from thicker yarn than the top*

Second, the **artistic possibilities** are unlimited. You can:

- *let stitch patterns cover the whole top of the foot, including the toe*
- *have access to the entire sock top as a unified design canvas*

Third, the **technical perspective**; the construction, once understood, is straightforward, simple, and versatile. You can:

- *knit the whole sock in the round, except for some short rows around the sole toe*
- *avoid picking up stitches entirely*
- *avoid Kitchener stitch entirely (unless you really like it)*
- *try a sock on to check fit at any point after about twelve rounds of toe shaping*
- *end the socks at any point after about twelve rounds of toe shaping, to make footlets, anklets, calf-length socks, or knee-highs*

Fourth, the method encourages **economy** in the use of both yarn and knitting time. You can:

- *make thrifty use of leftover yarns by knitting soles with them, because the sole doesn't have to be the same color or even the same gauge as the rest of the sock*
- *make the legs as short or as long as your yarn quantity allows (an advantage shared with toe-up construction)*
- *keep a supply of soles knitted up in advance, to await need or inspiration*

And, finally, for those who enjoy having a **philosophical context** for knitting, you can:

- *have the satisfaction of adhering to the principle that "form follows function" by knitting the sole in a way that reflects its unique shape and function*

You see that this solefull architecture has many impressive possibilities. But you know there are other architectures out there. You've probably already knitted socks from the top down, toe up, or side-to-side, as I have. Maybe you've even experimented with knitting the sole separately, as in Elizabeth Zimmermann's moccasin socks (*Knitter's Almanac*), Anna Zilboorg's free-sole socks (*Magnificent Mittens and Socks*), or Daniel Yuhas' heel-up socks (*Knitting from the Center Out*). My solefull sock architecture is another option, not meant to replace existing architectures but to offer a new set of solutions to some common sock problems.

Let me show you how I found my way to it.

My Journey of Discovery

My first efforts to prevent holes in my sock soles were on conventional architectures: top-down and toe-up. My firm goal was to make the solution functional, practical, and economical.

I tried extending the reinforcement yarn up to about mid-arch, but that looked funny on top and made the socks thicker right where my shoes tend to be tightest. So I tried carrying the reinforcement yarn only on the sole of each round at the ball of the foot, by using an intarsia-in-the-round technique. That was tedious and fiddly, and it left loose stitches at the edges of the reinforced area. I could have cut the reinforcement yarn after knitting the sole part of each round, but that seemed wasteful and kind of messy, with all those loose ends to either leave hanging or sew in.

I realized that the obvious solution was to knit the sole by itself; then I could reinforce the whole thing, easily and efficiently. I should confess right now that this was when

I became seriously addicted to carrying along a thin strand of a mohair/silk yarn for reinforcement. It adds warmth, softness, and strength without significantly increasing bulk. And it just feels so good, while both knitting it and wearing it!

I began this phase of experiments by provisionally casting on enough stitches for the perimeter of the sole (the outline of the foot as it stands on the ground), knitting in the round while decreasing at toe and heel, then ending by grafting (working Kitchener stitch) down the center of the sole. With the whole sole constructed, I put the provisional stitches at the perimeter on a circular needle and finished the sock top. However, this didn't fit the "functional" part of my goal. I didn't like having to stop and reverse directions, or to cut the yarn and join it again. I wanted a more elegant structural sequence.

So I tried working in the opposite direction: I started from a line of provisionally cast-on stitches at the center of the sole and worked out in the round to the perimeter. This was much simpler, and it allowed me to cut the reinforcement yarn just once, at the end of the sole, with no waste. I was on to something.

The next question was how to proceed from the sole perimeter onward to make the rest of the sock. At first I formed the top of the toe and foot by working back and forth while joining the first and last stitches of each row to the live sole stitches. That's how I constructed the Leopard Spot socks and Budapest Roof Tile socks, which I developed in 2008 and entered in the contest that resulted in their publication in *Think Outside the Sox* (XRX, Inc.). After I sent those socks to the contest, I kept tinkering with the architecture because I envisioned a workflow that would be even more natural and more intuitive. I really wanted to just keep knitting up in the round on all the perimeter stitches. I imagined the knitting proceeding exactly like water covers your foot when you step into a warm bath, both literally and figuratively knitting from the ground up.

This is where I really started getting excited, because doors to fascinating design possibilities began opening. I found that I could, indeed, shape the toe while knitting continuously in the round by using any number of intriguing decrease arrangements. What's more, those arrangements could be chosen to complement the stitch pattern! However, to make the foot fit right, I then needed to get rid of a lot of stitches all in one round. When working plain designs I could get past this hurdle by grafting them away (that is, using Kitchener stitch). However, grafting texture or color designs in pattern is fiddly at best, and crazy-making at worst.

The epiphany came in early 2009, when I devised what I called a *zip line* as a way to join the sides of the foot when they're long enough to meet in the middle. This zip line is really just a sequence of consecutive centered double decreases, where a center stitch is knitted together with one stitch from each side of the foot. It's a close relative of the three-needle bind-off, but it lies flatter. I've learned since that Daniel Yuhas has independently come up with a similar joining technique (*Knitting from the Center Out*), and even used the word "zip" in its description. This way of joining must be an idea whose time has come.

The zip line serves both structural and aesthetic functions. First, of course, it joins the sides of the foot to each other. As it turns out, it can also connect lines of toe-shaping decreases with the line of instep-shaping decreases, and this reveals a lot of design potential. When I began to test the possibilities of this technique, I was delighted by the way these intersecting shaping procedures interact with stitch patterns. They allow even simple color stripes to form intriguing new patterns.

Beyond the instep, a sock becomes a simple cylinder to enclose the leg, so my only development work in this section of the architecture was to devise calf-expansion options for those of us who need it. For those who don't, that expansion can be easily omitted.

The Possibilities Are Unlimited

Ironically, the thing that started this whole odyssey, that quest for a more durable sole, became almost a side effect. It was a valid and useful side effect, yes, but the kaleidoscopic effects that resulted when I applied color and texture to the structure became all-absorbing. Those effects make the toes and foot-tops so interesting, both to knit and to look at. After all, who sees our socks the most? We, the wearers, do — especially when we've kicked off our shoes and comfortably propped up our feet. And what part of them do we see the most? The top of the foot and toe. With solefull architecture, you can look forward to admiring the stitch patterns as they are transformed, almost magically, both while you work the structure on your needles and again, in a different way, when you put on the finished socks.

HOW DOES THE SOLEFULL STRUCTURE WORK?

Let's take a brief guided tour of solefull architecture. Later we will get into details. Some schematic drawings, which I think of as maps, will guide our progress.

The Sole

We start at the center of the sole with a line of provisionally cast-on stitches, as shown by the red line in Figure 1.

Round 1 (Figure 2), worked around all those stitches, makes a long, skinny oval. (BOR indicates the beginning of the round.) We keep working around in concentric ovals, making increases at the toe and heel to keep the fabric flat. Sole Toe and Sole Heel charts, included in each pattern, tell you where and how to work these increases.

Then, because the toes and ball of a human foot are wider than the heel, we knit a round that includes short rows around the toe and ball of the foot (Figure 3). After a few more plain rounds, we've reached the end of the sole.

The Sock Top

For the next phase we'll look at a different kind of map: a three-dimensional view of the sock top (Figure 4). It's color-coded to show the different structural areas. Because we're knitting from the ground up, we're now at the outer perimeter of the foot, at the very bottom of the blue area. We continue knitting in the round and our progress begins to move upward rather than outward. We make decreases in the toe area to

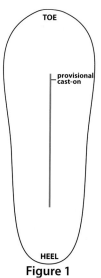

Figure 1

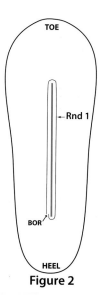

Figure 2

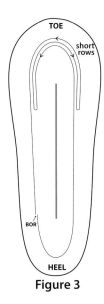

Figure 3

shape it. When we've knitted enough fabric along the sides to cover half the width of the foot, we join the two sides of the lower foot with a zip line, shown in bright pink on this diagram.

Now we've arrived at the instep (orange area). We shape the instep by working decreases at the center front.

Next comes the ankle (gray area), which is smooth sailing; we just go around and around with no shaping. The leg (green area) can continue in the same way, or you have the option of making increases to expand the calf.

Last comes the cuff (pink area).

Where to Next?

Okay. Regardless of your experience with knitting socks and reading charts, if you can knit in the round you now know enough to go forth and solefully knit the first two designs in the Stockinette chapter. While those designs do include two charts (for the Sole Toe and the Sole Heel), every round is also written out in words.

On the other hand, if you're an adventurous, experienced sock knitter and a chart devotee, you're probably good to go for any sock in the book.

If you want more information about the charts, proceed to The VIP Tour (page 14). If you have questions, check out the Details, Digressions, and Helpful Bits chapter (page 17).

Have fun on your own solefull sock journey!

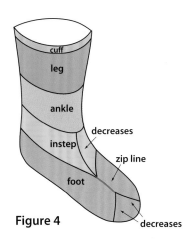

Figure 4

The VIP Tour of Solefull Architecture

You've had the introductory tour, so you know the basics. Now you're ready for a VIP tour of the charts and diagrams, should you choose to take it. You can always come back to it later if questions arise.

The Sole

It has two charts, one at the heel and one at the toe. They show where to increase and where to do short rows. Figure 5 shows those two charts laid over the sole outline that you saw earlier.

You'll notice two things right away:
- *The charts are straight at the top, while the outlines of the toe and heel are curves. That's because charts don't bend (except in JC Briar's Stitch Maps; see page 186), but knitting does.*
- *Each wedge-shaped chart in Figure 5 has a darker half and a lighter half. The darker half corresponds to the Sole Toe and Sole Heel charts that you see with each pattern. The lighter half is the mirror image that you'll work when you reach the center line and reverse your direction of chart reading.*

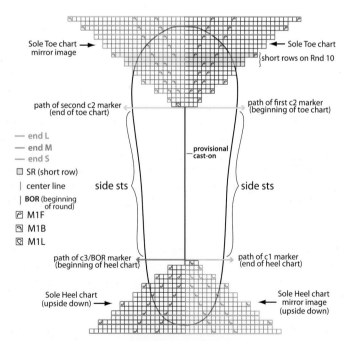

Figure 5 - Sole Outline with overlaid charts

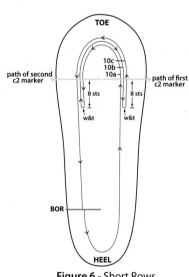

Figure 6 - Short Rows on Round 10

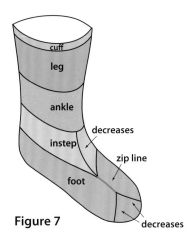

Figure 7

Look closely at the two halves of each chart. You'll see that they show mirrored increases: forward loop on the darker half and backward loop on the lighter half. *That is completely optional.* You can make all the sole increases by forward loops if you want, or all by backward loops — whatever is easier for you to make and to work into on the next round. It won't affect wear in the least either way, and even a purist would be hard-pressed to tell whether the increases were mirrored or not after you've worn the sock for a while and the sole has matted a bit. Plus, carrying along a mohair/silk yarn for reinforcement will obscure details like direction of increases even more.

Other things to note about Figure 5:
- *The markers (c1, c2, and c3) that you put in place on Rnd 1 of the sole are actually right at the beginning and end of the charts. The pink, yellow, and red arrows show the paths they take as you slip them on each round.*
- *The side stitches are not charted.*

On to Figure 6, which is all about the short rows needed at the toe end of the sole because the ball width of our feet is wider than the heel width. It shows you:
- *the path of each short row (a, b, and c)*
- *how the short rows extend past the c2 markers into the side sts*
- *how the short rows relate to the round on which they are done (Round 10)*

That's the end of the sole; follow me, please, to the next section.

The Top

Figure 7 may look familiar; it's the same as Figure 4 in the previous chapter. It's repeated here because it relates to Figures 8 and 9. Together they show how all the charts fit together.

Figure 8 is what you would get if you opened Figure 7 down the center back and front and laid it out flat. It's just like how map makers "cut" a globe at strategic places in order to show the whole world as a flat map. You aren't going to knit the sock flat, of course, but a two-dimensional diagram of the whole sock allows the chart shapes to be overlaid on it (Figure 9). That layout diagram is like a map of the charts, with arrows to points of interest. Vertical columns are repetitions of the stitch pattern chart, with the toe shaping chart between them. That lower part of the map is straightforward because the outline of the toe shaping chart on the map is the same shape as the actual toe shaping chart.

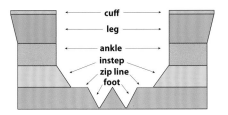

Figure 8

But above that the map gets a little less straightforward. Just as we had to cut Figure 7 at center front and back to open it out into FIgure 8, in order to make the Instep and Calf Shaping chart outlines fit our map we also have to cut them in two and show one half on each side (Figure 10).

The placement of the Instep chart halves on the map is uncomplicated because you work that whole chart from right to left. The halves migrate logically to their places on the map. But to work the Calf Shaping chart you actually start in the middle because that's where BOR is. Then you proceed to the left side of the chart as usual. The other half of the Calf Shaping chart, also worked from right to left, comes *after* the required stitch pattern repeats and finishes the round.

The main thing to note from all this is that even though the map (chart layout diagram) has open areas and split charts, the knitting doesn't; you do knit the whole sock top in the round.

That completes your VIP tour. You now have an insider's view of solefull sock structure. If you want to know more, the next chapter contains various minutiae, arranged alphabetically, for your perusal now or reference later.

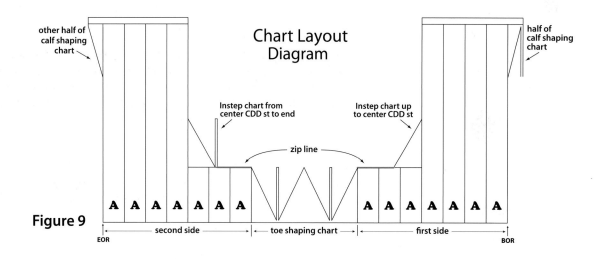

Figure 9

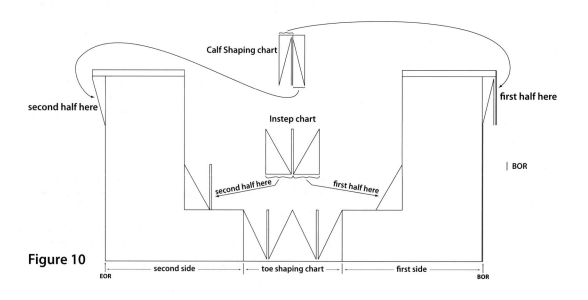

Figure 10

Details, Digressions, and Helpful Bits

This chapter is not required reading. It just explains stuff that might be interesting. But if you get stuck or have a question, check to see if the answer is here.

ankle fit
Rather than trying to keep my socks up via a tight cuff, I find it works better to "push" the tops up from below by making the ankle semi-fitted. The ankle can't be tight, of course, or the sock will be hard to get on. I try to keep the ankle just snug, then increase for the calf if needed.

You can accommodate thicker ankles by doing fewer centered double decreases (CDDs) at the instep. If you do, you'll also want to slow down the frequency of the last few instep CDDs; that is, you'll put more plain rounds between decrease rounds. In doing so you will depart from the Instep chart or instructions, of course, but the stitch pattern will be well enough established by then that you can read your knitting to see what comes next.

aphorisms
I'm known in my family for spouting aphorisms. I chose some for this book which relate to innovation and perseverance, the qualities mentioned in my dedication (page 3). They are in no particular order.

blocking
It's always knitter's choice whether to block or not, but I find that lace designs, at least, do benefit from this extra step. Also, designs where the stockinette stitch sole meets a largely purl sock top (such as Purl Parallelograms, Traveling Trellis, and Semi Aran) will want a little steam-blocking right at that transition area.

cast-on
The reason to start Judy's Magic Cast-On (JMCO) on the bottom needle point rather than the top one is so that the first stitch of Round 1 is the second-to-last, rather than last, stitch to be cast on. Starting that way discourages a little hole from forming at the beginning of Round 1.

CDD ridge
The slight ridges formed by lines of centered double decreases (CDDs) at toe and instep are on the outside of the sock, not against the foot. For super-sensitive feet, however, you can substitute a wider and slightly flatter decrease — ssk, k1, k2tog — for the CDD (see Irises, page 70). For placement purposes, this version is worked on five stitches, rather than three, and the k1 between the single decreases coincides with the center stitch of the CDD.

chart minutiae — some obvious, some not

BOR Placement: Beginning of round (BOR) is *between* the last and first stitches of the round, not *the* first stitch of the round. On some charts BOR and EOR are shown as two different lines to clarify chart usage. In reality, of course, they are at the exact same place on the actual knitting because all the knitting is in the round.

Chart Layout Diagrams: These are *not* strictly proportional to the finished socks.

Chart Symbols:
1. They are designed to depict how the knitting looks on the righthand needle (RN) after *completing* the operation the symbol stands for.
2. Execute them in the yarn color of the chart square they're on.

Lopsided Charts: Don't worry if some of the toe, instep, or calf charts look uneven; rest assured that the shaping they show is all centered at the front and/or back of the sock. Some of those charts are wider on one side to improve the flow to the next chart or to simplify instructions.

Marker Placement: Each square is a stitch. If a marker arrow points to the line between two stitches, the marker goes between those two stitches. If a marker arrow points to the middle of a square, i.e., to a single stitch, that means you will put a marker (pin-type) right on that stitch.

Quantity: Yes, there are *many* charts in most of the patterns. But you don't have to look at all of them — only the ones for your size, and then only the ones for the section you're actually working on. And once you get the pattern established you won't need the charts much.

Stitch Counts: The stitch counts are given on some charts (mostly the Sole Toe and Sole Heel charts) as an aid to catching errors, especially missed or extra increases.

color carries, vertical

The beginning of round for the whole sock top is at the center back, so colors carried up there from round to round are nicely out of the way. Remember two things: 1) keep the floats loose enough to match the vertical stretch of the rest of the sock and 2) twist the carried colors with the working color about every four rounds.

color choice

Be careful about choosing dark or busily variegated yarn for textured designs built on purls or traveling stitches; strongly contrasting or dark colors can obscure stitch patterns.

color coding for sizes

Many knitters prudently go through the instructions before they start a project and highlight the relevant numbers for their size. My goal in having those numbers printed in a different color for each size was to save you that step.

cord bind-off

This makes a neat, strong, and durable cuff for socks, but on a stockinette stitch fabric it can curl outward a little. If that is a problem, you might want to choose a ribbed or seed stitch cuff instead.

The total length of the cord needs to equal the circumference of the last sock round and have the same stretchiness. To that end, you can go up a needle size to work the cord, or increase sock stitches by 10% on the last round before working the cord, or just be conscious of working the cord at a looser-than-normal tension.

cuff options

I consider cuff options for most of these designs pretty much interchangeable; that's why some of the pairs show a different cuff on each sock. I wanted you to be able to see how different options look, as an aid to making your own choices.

Fair Isle (color stranding)

Be sure to keep the floats loose enough for good elasticity, especially on the leg. If in doubt, go up one needle size on the leg; working a slightly looser fabric won't affect wear on the leg as it would on the foot.

grafted foot join

There's no way to avoid the half-stitch offset when you graft the two sections of the foot together. As a result, even if you go to the trouble of grafting in pattern, the stitch patterns of the two sides still won't match up precisely. With a zip-line foot join, the stitch patterns of the two sides can match up exactly (divided by the zip line itself, of course).

Nonetheless, grafting in plain stockinette stitch will work well on these designs: Let the Yarn Shine, Shaded Golden Ratio, Canyon Walls, Balanced Biases, and Flaming Arrows.

heel and toe on lace designs

As tempting as it is to let a lace pattern stitch cover the whole sock top, this really isn't practical. That's why I don't start lace pattern stitches at the toe area until a few rounds have been knitted; this slight delay keeps toenails from poking through the lace.

For the heel area, I've shown two options: leaving it in stockinette stitch (Lace Trellis, page 150) or reinforcing it with Long Heel Stitch (Meandering Mesh, page 158, and Twining Vines, page 168).

heel reinforcement

On any of the plain stockinette stitch designs you can reinforce the back of the heel with Long Heel Stitch (page 182). Decide how wide you want the reinforced area to be and place stitch markers on each side. End the reinforcement stitch a little above shoe height. (See note about Long Heel Stitch, below.)

instep fit

For a low instep, add about two more stitches to the foot join and/or speed up the rate of the first few instep centered double decreases (CDDs) by working fewer plain rounds between decrease rounds. Be sure to try the sock on frequently to check fit.

For a high instep, subtract about two stitches from the foot join and/or slow down the rate of the first few instep CDDs by working more plain rounds between decrease rounds. Be sure to try the sock on frequently to check fit.

As with ankle changes (above), either of these adjustments will require you to read your knitting (not difficult, because the stitch pattern is already well established) to see how to continue in pattern.

jog handling

I've found the simplest way of handling color jogs in stripes is about as effective as any of the more complicated techniques. Do nothing on the first round of the new color. At the beginning of the second round of that color, lift the stitch of the round below (old color) onto the left needle and knit it together with the first stitch of the round. The location of the beginning of the round (BOR) does not change.

lace minutiae, namely ktbl

Knitting through the back of the loop (working a ktbl) on the *second* round directly above a yarn-over (YO) in the Lace Trellis charts (page 155) makes the stitch above the yarn-over neater. If the ktbl is not worked, that stitch spreads a little. Doing a similar ktbl isn't necessary on Meandering Mesh, however, because the stitch directly above the yarn-over is always involved in a decrease. It also isn't necessary on Twining Vines because the stockinette stitch sections slant obliquely, which counteracts the tendency of the stitch in question to spread.

ladders at needle intersections

To keep the tension even at needle intersections and discourage "ladders" in the knitted fabric from forming there, it helps to work the first stitch on the new needle normally, the second stitch tightly, the third stitch just snugly, then return to normal tension.

Ladders tend to be more of a problem when the yarn is a bit thin in relation to needle size.

lifted increase on sole, the one and only

The reason the increase at the toe in round 1 is worked as a M1L (lift and twist left), rather than M1F (forward loop) like all the rest of the increases on the sole, is because the M1L helps to correct any looseness in the stitch before it, which was the first cast-on stitch on the top needle.

Long Heel Stitch

The double wrap on this heel stitch (see page 182) keeps its vertical (round) gauge the same as the rest of the sock top, as is necessary with solefull architecture. With top-down architecture, where the heel flap is knitted separately, the vertical gauge of heel stitch doesn't have to match the rest of the sock.

lopsided sole heel — not

When you read the instruction on the last (or second-to-last, in some cases) sole round telling you to knit from the beginning of the round (BOR) to the center heel, you may think that this will make the heel lopsided because it will have one more round on one side than on the other. Not so; knitting to center heel at that point compensates for what was done at the very beginning of the sole, when round 1 (the set-up round) started at the center heel but round 2 and the rest of the sole rounds started at the first heel marker.

mirrored increases on the sole

For efficiency and space conservation, the Sole Heel and Sole Toe charts show M1F for all the increases. The same holds true where the sole instructions are written out round-by-round (pages 28 and 32). As explained in The VIP Tour (page 14), however, you can mirror the increases if you like — that is, use M1B in place of M1F — on the other side of center line in Sole Toe and Sole Heel charts. It won't affect wear either way and the bottom of the sole has very low visibility.

needles

Many knitting operations, such as double decreases and crossed stitches, are easier with well-tapered needle tips, such as those on Addi Lace needles.

For devotees of double-pointed needles, it really is easier to work Judy's Magic Cast-On (JMCO) and the first couple of sole rounds on one long circular needle or two shorter circular needles. After that, double-pointed needles work fine.

In the instructions for the sole set-up round, "Needle 1" and "Needle 2" refer either to the two ends of one long circular needle or to two shorter circular needles.

reinforcement yarn

The mohair/silk blend that I like so well as a reinforcement yarn doesn't felt on the sole over time, as I thought it would, but it does reinforce well and comfortably. Lucy Neatby calls mohair "nature's nylon," and in my experience that is true.

I've read that wooly nylon serger thread can be carried along with sock yarn for reinforcement purposes; this might be worth a try if you happen to have some around.

reknitting the sole, the easy way

1. Follow the same sole instructions you originally used for the sock from the cast-on through the second-to-last round.
2. Loosely sew down the live stitches to the perimeter of the old sole, leaving the old sole in place.

reknitting the sole, the invisible way

1. Follow the same sole instructions you originally used for the sock from the cast-on through the *fourth*-to-last round.
2. Remove the old sole as follows: Snip a stitch in its second-to-last round, unpick that round and capture the live loops of the sole perimeter on a needle as you go.

Note: Those loops will be from the last round of the old sole.

3. Count the live loops that you just mounted on the needle.

4. Work one more round on the new sole, distributing any needed increases around toe and heel to make the total stitch count match that of the mounted loops.

5. Graft (Kitchener stitch) the new sole to the old sole.

separate strand for foot join

If you are using variegated yarn, you have a decision to make about color for the foot join. You can just take the color that happens to be at the end of a ball, or you can cut out a strand in the color you prefer. If you end up deciding to cut your working yarn to adjust color placement, you might want to leave the cut end long enough to finish a full round.

size

If in doubt about which of two sizes to make, opt for the smaller one. In general, you want some negative ease in a sock.

smoother sole

If the feet you're knitting for need an extra smooth surface to walk on, you can reverse the knitting direction on the first round of the top so that the smooth (knit) side of the stockinette stitch sole will be against the bottom of the foot. This is especially important if you're using worsted weight yarn for the sole. The sock *top* will still have the knit side out (visible) as usual. Do a wrap and turn (w&t, page 185) when you reverse direction to prevent a little hole there.

spelling of "solefull"

You're right, one "l" would be the usual spelling in the suffix of that word, but I used two to emphasize that the sole is knitted in full in a special way. It just seemed that a new architecture should have a new word to go with it.

sole yarn amount

For purposes of reknitting a sole or using up dabs of leftover sock yarn for soles, here is a guideline for amount needed: each sole of a woman's size medium sock needs about 40 yards, or 9 grams, of fingering-weight sock yarn.

traveling stitches

The stitch columns that travel always consist of a single knit stitch on a background of purls, so knitting all of these through the back loop (tbl), including the crosses, really neatens them up. Purl stitches can be worked normally, through the front loop. It's worth learning to do the crosses without a cable needle because there are a lot of them.

trellis quartet

In the early days of developing solefull architecture, I wanted to prove to myself that the approach was viable for a variety of knitting techniques. So I rendered the same simple design motif — an all-over trellis — in purl stitches (page 44), Fair Isle (page 100), traveling stitch (page 124), and lace (page 150).

twist stitch methods

There are several ways to work twist stitches (crossing one stitch over one adjacent stitch) and you may already have your own favorite method. For me, the methods which leave one stitch on the left needle while the other is being worked stretch out both stitches a little. I use techniques which reverse the order of the stitches as I knit them, thus preventing either stitch from stretching. See page 182 for two types of Left Cross (LC) and page 183 for two types of Right Cross (RC).

working the wraps produced on sole short rows

It's easy to miss working the wraps along with the appropriate stitches on the round after they are made. A good preventive for that is to stop a few stitches after making a wrap and mark it with a pin. If you do miss a wrap anyway, be reassured that it will show very little on the sole and affect wear not at all.

zip line ridge

The slight ridge formed by the zip line is on the *outside* of the sock, not against your foot, so the vast majority of people will never feel it when wearing shoes. For extra-sensitive feet, however, you can opt to graft the foot join instead. But see grafted foot join, page 19, for more about that.

STOCKINETTE

Let the Yarn Shine

Here is the easiest way to get a fascinating, one-of-a-kind pair of solefull socks. Let a gorgeous long-repeat or no-repeat variegated yarn do its own thing, forming horizontal layers of color as you knit along in plain stockinette stitch. The layers don't even have to match on the two socks. In fact, with no-repeat variegated yarn they can't match precisely. The same colors will appear on each sock but the segments will be in different places. Whether your socks are fraternal twins or identical ones, magic happens when you put them on. Those parallel strata morph into surprising undulations of color around your toe and instep.

Yarn
Shown here:
- **Schoppel Wolle Crazy Zauberball**; 75% virgin wool / 25% nylon; 3.5 oz [100g], 460 yds [420 meters]; 1 (1, 2) balls ombre 1702 (MC)
- **Rowan Kidsilk Haze (optional reinforcement for sole)**; 70% super kid mohair / 30% silk; 0.88 oz [25g], 230 yds [210 meters]; color 629; about 0.28 oz [8g] needed for women's medium

Needles
Change needle size if necessary to get the gauge given.
- US size 1½ [2.5mm] — your choice: one long circular at least 40" [100cm], two shorter circulars, or dpns
- one dpn US size 1½ [2.5mm] — not needed if you're already using dpns

Notions
- stitch markers (2 pin-type, 4 any type in 3 colors: c1, c2, c3), tapestry needle

Gauge
- with reinforcing yarn on sole: 32 sts = 4" [10cm], 40 rnds = 4" [10cm]
- without reinforcing yarn, in pattern, unblocked: 34 sts = 4" [10cm], 42 rnds = 4" [10cm]

Size
small (S) - sole about 8.75" [22cm] long, for women's US shoe size 5-6 [Eur size 35/36]
medium (M) - sole about 9.5" [24cm] long, for women's US shoe size 7-8 [Eur size 37/38]
large (L) - sole about 10.25" [26cm] long, for women's US shoe size 9-10 [Eur size 39/40]

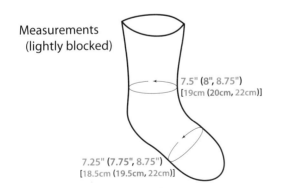

Measurements
(lightly blocked)

7.5" (8", 8.75")
[19cm (20cm, 22cm)]

7.25" (7.75", 8.75")
[18.5cm (19.5cm, 22cm)]

> "
> Confidence comes not from always being right but from not fearing to be wrong.
>
> Peter T. McIntyre
> "

SOLE

Holding MC and reinforcement yarn (optional) together and using a variation of JMCO (page 181), cast on 46 (50, 54) pairs of sts on 2 needle points. Total 92 (100, 108) sts.

Rnd 1 (set-up):

Needle 1: K1, M1F, k1, pm c1 for end of heel, k41 (45, 49), pm c2 for beginning of toe, k3. Needle 2: K1, M1L, k1, pm c2 for end of toe, k41 (45, 49), pm c3 for beginning of heel and BOR (3 sts remain on LN after BOR marker). There are 6 heel sts, 6 toe sts, and 41 (45, 49) sts on each side. Total 94 (102, 110) sts.

If you're working from charts, continue to **Rnds 2 - 13 (15, 17)**. If you're working without charts, go to **Sole in other words.***

Rnds 2 - 13 (15, 17):

Work Sole Heel chart between c3 and c1 markers, k41 (45, 49) side sts, work Sole Toe chart between c2 markers including SRs (page 184) as shown, and k41 (45, 49) side sts. Remove markers on last rnd. Then k17 (20, 22) to center heel (new BOR for rest of sock). Cut reinforcing yarn. Total 154 (172, 190) sts. Go to Foot.

*SOLE IN OTHER WORDS

Rnd 2:

M1F, k6, M1F, sl m, k41 (45, 49), sl m, M1F, k6, M1F, sl m, k41 (45, 49), sl BOR m. Total 98 (106, 114) sts.
Odd numbered rnds 3 - 11 (13, 15): Knit.

Rnd 4:

M1F, k2, M1F, (k1, M1F, k2, M1F) 2 times, sl m, k41 (45, 49), sl m, M1F, k2, M1F, (k1, M1F, k2, M1F) 2 times, sl m, k41 (45, 49), sl BOR m. Total 110 (118, 126) sts.

Rnd 6:

(M1F, k3) 2 times, M1F, k2, (M1F, k3) 2 times, M1F, sl m, k41 (45, 49), sl m, M1F, k4, M1F, (k1, M1F, k4, M1F) 2 times, sl m, k41 (45, 49), sl BOR m. Total 122 (130, 138) sts.

Rnd 8:

(k4, M1F) 4 times, k4, sl m, k41 (45, 49), sl m, (k6, M1F, k1, M1F) 2 times, k6, sl m, k41 (45, 49), sl BOR m. Total 130 (138, 146) sts.

Rnd 10:

M1F, k5, M1F, k4, M1F, k6, M1F, k4, M1F, k5, M1F, sl m, k41 (45, 49), sl m. Do SRs around toe as follows: K7, M1F, k1, M1F, k8, M1F, k1, M1F, k7, sl m, k8, w&t, p8, sl m, p28, sl m, p8, w&t, k8, sl m, M1F, k8, M1F, (k4, M1F) 3 times, k8, M1F, sl m, k41 (45, 49), sl BOR m. Total 146 (154, 162) sts.

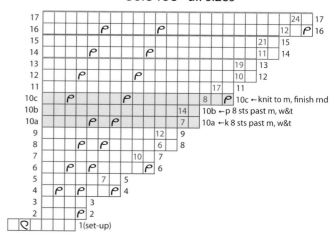

Sole Toe - all sizes

10c ← knit to m, finish rnd
10b ← p 8 sts past m, w&t
10a ← k 8 sts past m, w&t

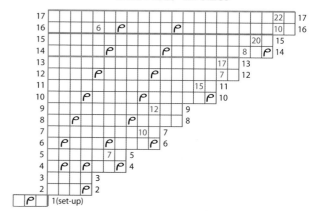

Sole Heel - all sizes

☐ k on RS, p on WS — end L
ℙ M1F — end M
ℚ M1L — end S
▨ short row | center line
  | **BOR** (beginning of round)

Chart notes:

Brown numbers give stitch counts greater than 5 to next symbol or end of chart.

After set-up round, work each row of chart twice; first from right to left, then from left to right.

OPTIONAL: When working from left to right, use M1B instead of M1F.

Rnd 12:
K7, M1F, k4, M1F, k8, M1F, k4, M1F, k7, sl m, k41 (45, 49), sl m, k10, M1F, k4, M1F, k6, M1F, k4, M1F, k10, sl m, k41 (45, 49), sl BOR m. Total 154 (162, 170) sts.

Rnd 13 (last rnd for S):
For sizes M and L: Knit. *For size S:* Removing markers as you go, knit to BOR, then k17 to center heel (new BOR for rest of sock). Cut reinforcing yarn. Total 154 sts. Go to Foot.

Rnd 14:
M1F, k8, M1F, k4, M1F, k10, M1F, k4, M1F, k8, M1F, sl m, k45 (49), sl m, k11, M1F, k4, M1F, k8, M1F, k4, M1F, k11, sl m, k45 (49), sl BOR m. Total 172 (180) sts.

Rnd 15 (last rnd for M):
For size L: Knit. *For size M:* Removing markers as you go, knit to BOR, then k20 to center heel (new BOR for rest of sock). Cut reinforcing yarn. Total 172 sts. Go to Foot.

Rnd 16:
K10, M1F, k4, M1F, k12, M1F, k4, M1F, k10, sl m, k49, sl m, M1F, k12, M1F, k4, M1F, k10, M1F, k4, M1F, k12, M1F, sl m, k49, sl BOR m. Total 190 sts.

Rnd 17 (last rnd for L):
Knit to BOR removing markers as you go, then k22 to center heel (new BOR for rest of sock). Cut reinforcing yarn. Total 190 sts. Go to Foot.

FOOT
Toe Shaping
Mark 12th (13th, 14th) st on each side of center front. These stitches are the centers of CDDs which shape the toe.

Odd numbered rnds 1 - 21: Knit.

Even numbered rnds 2 - 22 and Rnd NA (23, 23-24): (knit to 1 st before marked st, CDD) 2 times, knit to end of rnd. Total 110 (124, 138) sts remain.

ZIP LINE
Rnd 23 (24, 25): Knit 42 (46, 50) sts.
Join sides of lower foot: Drop working yarn and sl next 12 (15, 18) sts to RN. [If using circular needle(s), don't pull sts on RN to the cable yet.] Sl next 14 (17, 20) sts to dpn (temporary LN). Cut a separate strand of yarn about 18" long. Leaving a 4" tail,

k2tog with separate strand. Slip st just made back to LN without turning it. Then make a zip line up the foot with that separate strand by doing the following three steps 11 (14, 17) times:
1. sl 1 st from RN to LN
2. CDD with next 3 sts
3. sl st just made back to LN

Then do step 1 again, drop the separate strand, pick up MC working yarn and do last zip CDD with it.

Finish rnd with working yarn. Total 85 (93, 101) sts remain.

INSTEP
Use a pin to mark center front stitch coming from zip line and position it as first st on LN. It will be the center of instep-shaping CDDs. See page 179 for handling a CDD that spans a needle intersection.

Rnds 24-27 (25-29, 26-30):
Knit to 1 st before marked st, CDD, knit to end of rnd. Total 77 (83, 91) sts.
Even numbered rnds 28-40 (30-42, 32-44): Knit.
Odd numbered rnds 29-41 (31-43, 31-45): Knit to 1 st before marked st, CDD, knit to end of rnd. Total 63 (69, 75) sts remain.

ANKLE
Knit 63 (69, 75) sts on each rnd until sock measures 5.5" (6", 6.5") [14cm (15cm, 16.5cm)] above sole.

LEG
Decide whether you need calf expansion (see page 179 for options). If not, work as for ankle for about 1.5" (2", 2.5") [4cm (5cm, 6.5cm)] or desired length.

Calf expansion by st increases: K1, M1B, knit to 1 st before end of rnd, M1F, end k1. Do this every 5th rnd 5 times. Knit 73 (79, 85) sts on each rnd for about 1" or length desired.

CUFF
Finish socks with cuff of your choice; see page 180 for options. Cuffs on sample are 4-st cord BO.

FINISHING
Sew in yarn tails on WS, snugging up last st of zip line with tail hanging there.

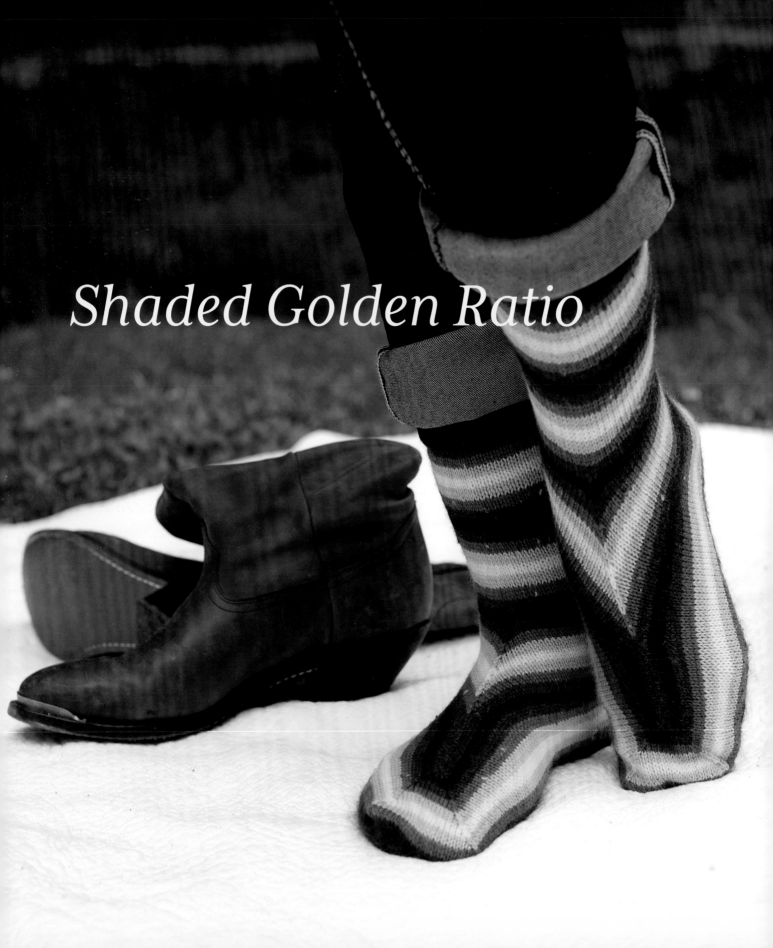

Shaded Golden Ratio

Art meets math here. The golden ratio means that when the parts of a composition have a ratio of approximately 3:5 to each other and to the whole, the design will look pleasingly balanced. On these socks, the light-colored stripes are three units high (a unit = three rounds) and the dark ones are five units high. Both the light and dark stripes incorporate color bands that are graduated in value. Any five light-to-dark values of the same hue can be used. Further interest is provided if the middle value, the one used most often, is a tweed, marled, or heather yarn.

Measurements
(lightly blocked)

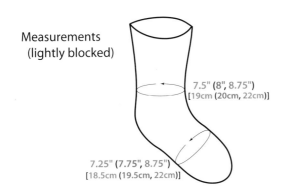

7.5" (8", 8.75")
[19cm (20cm, 22cm)]

7.25" (7.75", 8.75")
[18.5cm (19.5cm, 22cm)]

Yarn
Shown here:
- **Berroco Ultra Alpaca Fine;** 50% Peruvian Wool / 20% Super FIne Alpaca / 30% Nylon; 3.5 oz [100 g], 433 yds [400 meters]; 1 (1, 1) skein 1279 (MC)
- **Regia 4-Fach Haltbar;** 75% Superwash New Wool / 25% Polyamid; 1.75 oz [50g], 230 yds [210 meters]; 1 (1, 1) ball 1992 (CC1)
- **Lorna's Laces Shepard Sock;** 80% Superwash wool / 20% polyamide; 1.75 oz [50g], 215 yds [197 meters]; 1 (1, 1) skein Chino (CC2)
- **Knit Picks Essential Tweed;** 65% Superwash Wool / 25% nylon / 10% Donegal; 1.75 oz [50g], 231 yds [211 meters]; 1 (1, 1) ball Inca Gold (CC3)
- **Lorna's Laces Shepard Sock;** 80% Superwash wool / 20% polyamide; 1.75 oz [50g], 215 yds [197 meters]; 1 (1, 1) skein Charcoal (CC4)
- **Rowan Kidsilk Haze (optional reinforcement for sole);** 70% super kid mohair / 30% silk; 0.88 oz [25g], 230 yds [210 meters]; color 584; about 0.28 oz [8g] needed for women's medium

Needles
Change needle size if necessary to get the gauge given.
- US size 1½ [2.5mm] — your choice: one long circular at least 40" [100cm], two shorter circulars, or dpns
- one dpn US size 1½ [2.5mm] — not needed if you're already using dpns

Notions
- stitch markers (2 pin-type, 4 any type in 3 colors: c1, c2, c3), tapestry needle

Gauge
- with reinforcing yarn on sole: 32 sts = 4" [10cm], 40 rnds = 4" [10cm]
- without reinforcing yarn, in pattern, unblocked: 34 sts = 4" [10cm], 42 rnds = 4" [10cm]

Size
small (S) - sole about 8.75" [22cm] long, for women's US shoe size 5-6 [Eur size 35/36]

medium (M) - sole about 9.5" [24cm] long, for women's US shoe size 7-8 [Eur size 37/38]

large (L) - sole about 10.25" [26cm] long, for women's US shoe size 9-10 [Eur size 39/40]

SOLE

Holding MC and reinforcement yarn (optional) together and using a variation of JMCO (page 181), cast on 46 (50, 54) pairs of sts on 2 needle points. Total 92 (100, 108) sts.

Rnd 1 (set-up):
Needle 1: K1, M1F, k1, pm c1 for end of heel, k41 (45, 49), pm c2 for beginning of toe, k3. Needle 2: K1, M1L, k1, pm c2 for end of toe, k41 (45, 49), pm c3 for beginning of heel and BOR (3 sts remain on LN after BOR marker). There are 6 heel sts, 6 toe sts, and 41 (45, 49) sts on each side. Total 94 (102, 110) sts.

If you're working from charts, continue to **Rnds 2 - 13 (15, 17)**. If you're working without charts, go to **Sole in other words.***

Rnds 2 - 13 (15, 17):
Work Sole Heel chart between c3 and c1 markers, k41 (45, 49) side sts, work Sole Toe chart between c2 markers including SRs (page 184) as shown, and k41 (45, 49) side sts. Remove markers on last rnd. Then k17 (20, 22) to center heel (new BOR for rest of sock). Cut reinforcing yarn. Total 154 (172, 190) sts. Go to Foot.

*SOLE IN OTHER WORDS:

Rnd 2:
M1F, k6, M1F, sl m, k41 (45, 49), sl m, M1F, k6, M1F, sl m, k41 (45, 49), sl BOR m. Total 98 (106, 114) sts.
Odd numbered rnds 3 - 11 (13, 15): Knit.

Rnd 4:
M1F, k2, M1F, (k1, M1F, k2, M1F) 2 times, sl m, k41 (45, 49), sl m, M1F, k2, M1F, (k1, M1F, k2, M1F) 2 times, sl m, k41 (45, 49), sl BOR m. Total 110 (118, 126) sts.

Rnd 6:
(M1F, k3) 2 times, M1F, k2, (M1F, k3) 2 times, M1F, sl m, k41 (45, 49), sl m, M1F, k4, M1F, (k1, M1F, k4, M1F) 2 times, sl m, k41 (45, 49), sl BOR m. Total 122 (130, 138) sts.

Rnd 8:
(k4, M1F) 4 times, k4, sl m, k41 (45, 49), sl m, (k6, M1F, k1, M1F) 2 times, k6, sl BOR m. Total 130 (138, 146) sts.

Rnd 10:
M1F, k5, M1F, k4, M1F, k6, M1F, k4, M1F, k5, M1F, sl m, k41 (45, 49), sl m. Do SRs around toe as follows: K7, M1F, k1, M1F, k8, M1F, k1, M1F, k7, sl m, k8, w&t, p8, sl m, p28, sl m, p8, w&t, k8, sl m, M1F, k8, M1F, (k4, M1F) 3 times, k8, M1F, sl m, k41 (45, 49), sl BOR m. Total 146 (154, 162) sts.

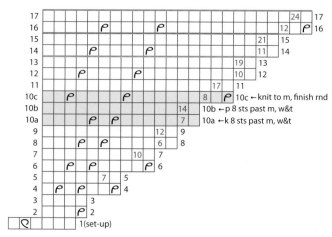

Sole Toe - all sizes

10c ← knit to m, finish rnd
10b ← p 8 sts past m, w&t
10a ← k 8 sts past m, w&t

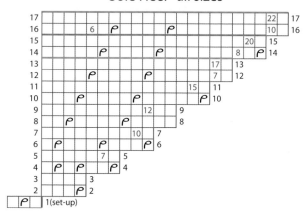

Sole Heel - all sizes

☐ k on RS, p on WS — end L
ℙ M1F — end M
ℚ M1L — end S
▨ short row | center line
| **BOR** (beginning of round)

Chart notes:
Brown numbers give stitch counts greater than 5 to next symbol or end of chart.

After set-up round, work each row of chart twice; first from right to left, then from left to right.

OPTIONAL: When working from left to right, use M1B instead of M1F.

Rnd 12:
K7, M1F, k4, M1F, k8, M1F, k4, M1F, k7, sl m, k41 (45, 49), sl m, k10, M1F, k4, M1F, k6, M1F, k4, M1F, k10, sl m, k41 (45, 49), sl BOR m. Total 154 (162, 170) sts.

Rnd 13 (last rnd for S):
For sizes M and L: Knit. For size S: Removing markers as you go, knit to BOR, then k17 to center heel (new BOR for rest of sock). Cut reinforcing yarn. Total 154 sts. Go to Foot.

Rnd 14:
M1F, k8, M1F, k4, M1F, k10, M1F, k4, M1F, k8, M1F, sl m, k45 (49), sl m, k11, M1F, k4, M1F, k8, M1F, k4, M1F, k11, sl m, k45 (49), sl BOR m. Total 172 (180) sts.

Rnd 15 (last rnd for M):
For size L: Knit. For size M: Removing markers as you go, knit to BOR, then k20 to center heel (new BOR for rest of sock). Cut reinforcing yarn. Total 172 sts. Go to Foot.

Rnd 16:
K10, M1F, k4, M1F, k12, M1F, k4, M1F, k10, sl m, k49, sl m, M1F, k12, M1F, k4, M1F, k10, M1F, k4, M1F, k12, M1F, sl m, k49, sl BOR m. Total 190 sts.

Rnd 17 (last rnd for L):
Knit to BOR removing markers as you go, then k22 to center heel (new BOR for rest of sock). Cut reinforcing yarn. Total 190 sts. Go to Foot.

FOOT
Color Pattern for sock top
3 rnds of each color in this order: *CC3, CC2, CC1, CC2, CC3, MC, CC4, MC, repeat from*. See page 20 for reducing color jog between stripes.

Toe Shaping
Mark 12th (13th, 14th) st on each side of center front. These stitches are the centers of CDDs which shape the toe.
Odd numbered rnds 1 - 21: Knit.
Even numbered rnds 2 - 22 and Rnd NA (23, 23-24): (knit to 1 st before marked st, CDD) 2 times, knit to end of rnd. Total 110 (124, 138) sts remain.

ZIP LINE
Rnd 23 (24, 25):
Knit 42 (46, 50) sts.

Join sides of lower foot: Drop working yarn and sl next 12(15,18) sts to RN. [If using circular needle(s), don't pull sts on RN to the cable yet.] Sl next 14 (17, 20) sts to dpn (temporary LN). Cut a separate strand of yarn about 18" long in the CC of rnd 22 (23, 25). Leaving a 4" tail, k2tog with separate strand. Slip st just made back to LN without turning it. Then make a zip line up the foot with that separate strand by doing the following three steps 11 (14, 17) times:
1. sl 1 st from RN to LN
2. CDD with next 3 sts
3. sl st just made back to LN

Then do step 1 again, drop the separate strand, pick up working yarn and do last zip CDD with it.

Finish rnd with working yarn. Total 85 (93, 101) sts remain.

INSTEP
Use a pin to mark center front stitch coming from zip line and position it as first st on LN. It will be the center of instep-shaping CDDs. See page 179 for handling a CDD that spans a needle intersection.

Rnds 24-27 (25-29, 26-30):
Knit to 1 st before marked st, CDD, knit to end of rnd. Total 77 (83, 91) sts.
Even numbered rnds 28-40 (30-42, 32-44): Knit.
Odd numbered rnds 29-41 (31-43, 31-45): Knit to 1 st before marked st, CDD, knit to end of rnd. Total 63 (69, 75) sts remain.

ANKLE
Knit 63 (69, 75) sts on each rnd until sock measures 5.5" (6", 6.5") [14cm (15cm, 16.5cm)] above sole.

LEG
Decide whether you need calf expansion (see page 179 for options). If not, work as for ankle for about 1.5" (2", 2.5") [4cm (5cm, 6.5cm)] or desired length.

Calf expansion by st increases: K1, M1B, knit to 1 st before end of rnd, M1F, end k1. Do this every 5th rnd 5 times. Knit 73 (79, 85) sts on each rnd for about 1" or length desired.

CUFF
Finish socks with cuff of your choice; see page 180 for options. If cuff will be a different color than last rnd worked, knit one full rnd in cuff color. Cuffs shown are 4-st cord BO (page 180) and 7 rnds of k1 tbl, p1 rib followed by JSSBO (page 181).

FINISHING
Sew in yarn tails on WS, snugging up last st of zip line with tail hanging there.

> "
> The best way to have a good idea is to have lots of ideas.
>
> Linus Pauling
> "

Canyon Walls

So far I haven't been to any canyons, even the Grand Canyon, but my impressions of their geologic features from photos inspired this design. The rich, warm colors of these yarns evoke sunlight on rock walls to me. And wearing the socks heightens the impression of rock strata even more, as the graduated stripes ripple and flow around the foot.

Measurements
(lightly blocked)

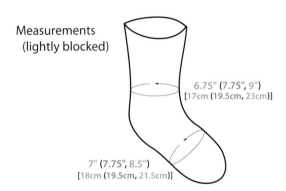

6.75" (7.75", 9")
[17cm (19.5cm, 23cm)]

7" (7.75", 8.5")
[18cm (19.5cm, 21.5cm)]

Notes

- There is lots of scope here for designing your own strata. You can, for example, vary their depth randomly or use more than two colors. And who's to say that the two socks must have identical strata? No two sections of real canyon walls are identical.
- Instructions are given here for joining the foot sides by zipping, but this design is equally suitable for grafting. I did one sock each way, just for comparison.
- There are extra lines of decreases in this toe shaping, so the color layers bend gradually around the toe in a way that evokes stratified rock walls.

Yarn

Shown here:
- **Mountain Colors Crazyfoot;** 90% Superwash Merino Wool / 10% nylon; 3.5 oz [100g], 425 yds [388 meters]; 1 (1, 1) skein Yellowstone (MC)
- **Blue Moon Socks that Rock;** 100% superwash merino - mediumweight; 5.5 oz [155g], 380 yds [347 meters]; 1 (1, 1) skein 24 Karat (CC)
- **Rowan Kidsilk Haze (optional reinforcement for sole);** 70% super kid mohair / 30% silk; 0.88 oz [25g], 230 yds [210 meters]; color 584; about 0.28 oz [8g] needed for women's medium

Needles

Change needle size if necessary to get gauge given.
- US size 1½ [2.5mm] — your choice: one long circular at least 40" [100cm], two shorter circulars, or dpns
- one dpn US size 1½ [2.5mm] — not needed if you're already using dpns

Notions

- stitch markers (3 pin-type, 4 any type in 3 colors: c1, c2, c3), tapestry needle

Gauge

- with reinforcing yarn on sole: 32 sts = 4" [10cm], 40 rnds = 4" [10cm]
- without reinforcing yarn, in pattern, unblocked: 29 sts = 4" [10cm], 45 rnds = 4" [10cm]

Size

small (S) - sole about 8.75" [22cm] long, for women's US shoe size 5-6 [Eur size 35/36]

medium (M) - sole about 9.5" [24cm] long, for women's US shoe size 7-8 [Eur size 37/38]

large (L) - sole about 10.25" [26cm] long, for women's US shoe size 9-10 [Eur size 39/40]

SOLE

Holding MC and reinforcement yarn (optional) together and using a variation of JMCO (page 181), cast on 44 (47, 51) pairs of sts on 2 needle points. Total 88 (94, 102) sts.

Rnd 1 (set-up):
Needle 1: K1, M1F, k1, pm c1 for end of heel, k39 (42, 46), pm c2 for beginning of toe, k3. Needle 2: K1, M1L, k1, pm c2 for end of toe, k39 (42, 46), pm c3 for beginning of heel and BOR (3 sts remain on LN after BOR marker). There are 6 heel sts, 6 toe sts, and 39 (42, 46) sts on each side. Total 90 (96, 104) sts.

Rnds 2 - 12 (14, 16):
Work Sole Heel chart between c3 and c1 markers, k39 (42, 46) side sts, work Sole Toe chart between c2 markers including SRs (page 184) as shown, and k39 (42, 46) side sts. Then k15 (17, 20) to center heel (new BOR for rest of sock). Total 142 (156, 174) sts.

Rnd 13 (15, 17):
Note: This round does not appear on Sole Toe and Sole Heel charts.

Removing markers as you go, adjust st count for sock top as follows:
Size S: k2, k2tog, (k5, k2tog) 4 times, (k6, k2tog) 9 times, (k5, k2tog) 5 times, end k3.
Size M: k5, k2tog, (k6, k2tog) 18 times, end k5.
Size L: k3, k2tog, (k6, k2tog) 7 times, (k7, k2tog) 6 times, (k6, k2tog) 7 times, end k3.

Cut reinforcing yarn. Total 123 (137, 153) sts.

Color Pattern for sock top: Design your own strata as described in the introduction, or use this sequence:
Rnds 1 - 13:
11 rnds CC, 2 rnds MC.
Rnds 14 - 26:
9 rnds CC, 4 rnds MC.
Rnds 27 - 39:
8 rnds CC, 5 rnds MC.
Rnds 40 - 52:
6 rnds CC, 7 rnds MC.
Rnds 53 - 65:
5 rnds CC, 8 rnds MC.
Rnds 66 - 78:
3 rnds CC, 10 rnds MC.
Rnds 79 - 91:
2 rnds CC, 11 rnds MC.

Sole Toe - all sizes

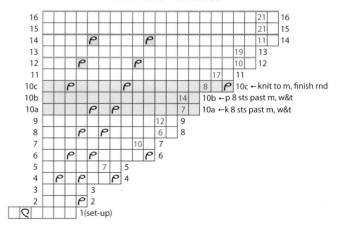

Sole Heel - all sizes

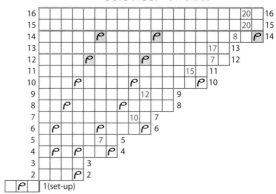

☐ k on RS, p on WS
⌐ M1F
⌐ M1L
| center line
| BOR (beginning of round)

— end L
— end M
— end S
▨ for size M only omit increases
▨ for size S only omit increases
▨ short row

Chart notes:
Brown numbers give stitch counts greater than 5 to next symbol or end of chart.

After set-up round, work each row of chart twice; first from right to left, then from left to right.

OPTIONAL: When working from left to right, use M1B instead of M1F.

For this design the natural color jog between stripes is very appropriate to the theme. But if you prefer to minimize it, see page 20. Either way, you can float the unused color(s) up the center back or cut them, as you like. Catch in the floats with the working color every 3 or 4 rnds, and keep them loose enough to let the back of the sock stretch normally.

FOOT

Toe Shaping Rnds 1 - 23 (24, 25):
Starting at center heel with CC, work as follows:
Knit 39 (46, 54), Toe Shaping chart (on first rnd place markers where indicated), knit 39 (46, 54). Note: See page 179 for handling a CDD that spans a needle intersection. Total 81 (95, 111) sts remain.

ZIP LINE

Rnd 24 (25, 26):
Knit 31 (36, 42) sts.
Join sides of lower foot: Drop working yarn and sl next 9 (11, 13) sts to RN. [If using circular needle(s), don't pull sts on RN to the cable yet.] Sl next 10 (12, 14) sts to dpn (temporary LN). Cut a separate strand of yarn about 18" long in the color of the rnd you're working. Leaving a 4" tail, make a zip line up the foot with that separate strand by doing the following three steps 8 (10, 12) times:
1. sl 1 st from RN to LN
2. CDD with next 3 sts
3. sl st just made back to LN

Then do step 1 again, drop the separate strand, pick up working yarn and do last zip CDD with it.

Finish rnd with working yarn. Total 63 (73, 85) sts remain.

INSTEP

Use a pin to mark center front stitch coming from zip line and position it as first st on LN. It will be the center of instep-shaping CDDs. See page 179 for handling a CDD that spans a needle intersection. Shape Instep as follows:
Rnds 25-26 (26-27, 27-29):
Knit, making a CDD at marked st every rnd. Total 59 (69, 79) sts remain.
Rnds 27-30 (28-33, 30-37):
Knit, making a CDD at marked st every other rnd. Total 55 (63, 71) sts remain.
Rnds 31-36 (34-39, 38-43):
Knit, making a CDD at marked st every third rnd. Total 51 (59, 67) sts remain.

Rnds 37-40 (40-43, 44-47):
Knit, making a CDD at marked st on rnd 40 (43, 47). Total 49 (57, 65) sts remain.

ANKLE

Knit 49 (57, 65) sts on each rnd until sock measures 5.5" (6", 6.5") [14cm (15cm, 16.5cm)] above sole.

LEG

Decide whether you need calf expansion (see page 179 for options). If not, work as for ankle for about 1.5" (2", 2.5") [4cm (5cm, 6.5cm)] or desired length.

Calf expansion by st increases: K1, M1B, knit to 1 st before end of rnd, M1F, end k1. Do this every 5th rnd 5 times. Knit 59 (67, 75) sts on each rnd for about 1" or length desired.

CUFF

Finish socks with cuff of your choice in either CC or MC; see page 180 for options. Cuffs shown are 4-st cord BO and five ridges of garter stitch in alternating CC and MC (one ridge = k one rnd, p next rnd in same color).

FINISHING

Sew in yarn tails on WS, snugging up last st of zip line with tail hanging there.

> "
> Uncertainty and mystery are energies of life... they keep boredom at bay and spark creativity.
> R.I. Fitzhenry
> "

Note: Use decrease symbols in black and color for your size only.
Treat as blank any squares which contain symbols for other sizes.

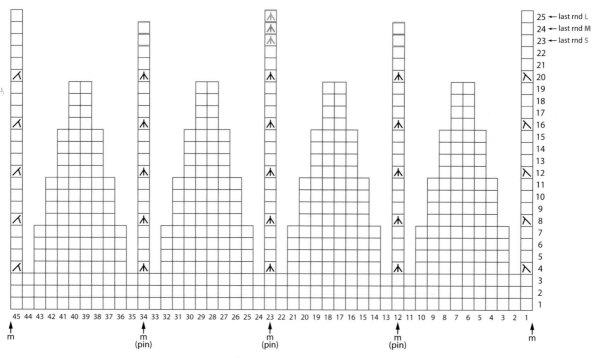

Toe Shaping - All Sizes

knit — end S

k2tog — end M

ssk — end L

(any color) CDD

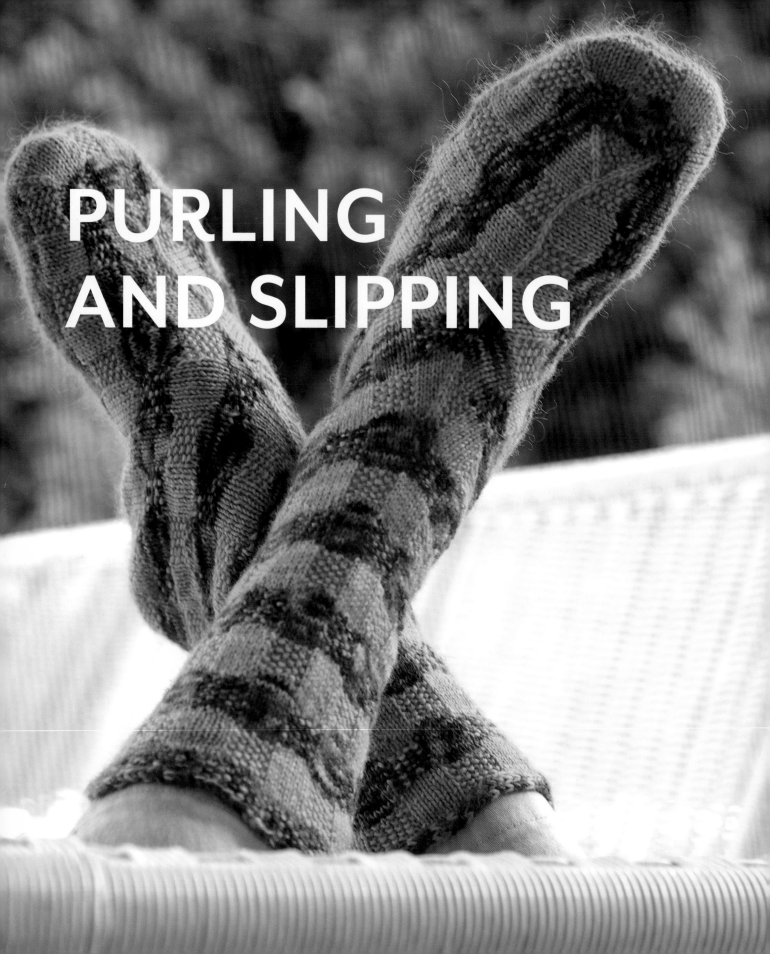

PURLING
AND SLIPPING

Purl Trellis

Meet the first member of the Trellis Quartet, the group of designs which were my testing ground for proving that solefull architecture works with a variety of patterning techniques. This knit/purl version is the easiest of the four, but the design can still hold its own even in this lively turquoise color. As you contemplate the toes of these socks, you may notice that the lattice lines form shapes other than diamonds (kites, for example) where they converge, due to the toe shaping and foot joining.

Measurements
(lightly blocked)

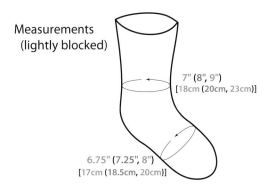

7" (8", 9")
[18cm (20cm, 23cm)]

6.75" (7.25", 8")
[17cm (18.5cm, 20cm)]

Note
● This design is best worked in a solid color, because even a mildly variegated yarn could obscure the pattern formed by the lines of single purl stitches. A medium or light color will be best; the turquoise shown is about as dark as you'd want to go.

Yarn
Shown here:
● **Cascade Yarns Heritage Sock Yarn;** 75% Merino Superwash / 25% Nylon; 3.5 oz [100 g], 400 meters [437 yds]; 1 (1, 2) skeins color 5626 (MC)
● **Rowan Kidsilk Haze (optional reinforcement for sole);** 70% super kid mohair / 30% silk; 0.88 oz [25g], 230 yds [210 meters]; color 632; about 0.28 oz [8g] needed for women's medium

Needles
Change needle size if necessary to get gauge given.
● US size 1½ [2.5mm] for sole with reinforcing yarn — your choice: one long circular at least 40" [100cm], two shorter circulars, or dpns
● US size 1 [2.25mm] for sock top — your choice: one long circular at least 40" [100cm], two shorter circulars, or dpns one dpn US size 1 [2.25mm] — not needed if you're already using dpns

Notions
● stitch markers (2 pin-type, 4 any type in 3 colors: c1, c2, c3), tapestry needle

Gauge
● with reinforcing yarn on sole: 32 sts = 4" [10cm], 40 rnds = 4" [10cm]
● without reinforcing yarn, in pattern, unblocked: 32 sts = 4" [10cm], 49 rnds = 4" [10cm]

Size
small (S) - sole about 8.75" [22cm] long, for women's US shoe size 5-6 [Eur size 35/36]
medium (M) - sole about 9.5" [24cm] long, for women's US shoe size 7-8 [Eur size 37/38]
large (L) - sole about 10.25" [26cm] long, for women's US shoe size 9-10 [Eur size 39/40]

SOLE

Holding MC and reinforcement yarn (optional) together and using a variation of JMCO (page 181), cast on 46 (50, 54) pairs of sts on 2 needle points. Total 92 (100, 108) sts.

Rnd 1 (set-up):
Needle 1: K1, M1F, k1, pm c1 for end of heel, k41 (45, 49), pm c2 for beginning of toe, k3. Needle 2: K1, M1L, k1, pm c2 for end of toe, k41 (45, 49), pm c3 for beginning of heel and BOR (3 sts remain on LN after BOR marker). There are 6 heel sts, 6 toe sts, and 41 (45, 49) sts on each side. Total 94 (102, 110) sts.

Rnds 2 - 12 (14, 16):
Work Sole Heel chart between c3 and c1 markers, k41 (45, 49) side sts, work Sole Toe chart between c2 markers including SRs (page 184) as shown, and k41 (45, 49) side sts. Then k17 (20, 22) to center heel (new BOR for rest of sock). Total 154 (172, 190) sts.

Rnd 13 (15, 17):
Note: This round does not appear on Sole Toe and Sole Heel charts. Removing markers as you go, adjust st count for sock top as follows:
Size S: k50, M1F, k54, M1F, end k50.
Size M: Knit.
Size L: k15, k2tog, k156, k2tog, end k15.

Cut reinforcing yarn. Total 156 (172, 188) sts.

FOOT

Toe Shaping
Refer to Chart Layout diagram for your size. From center heel BOR with 2.25mm needle, work as follows:

Rnd 1 (set-up):
First side: Chart A 6 (7, 8) times. Total 48 (56, 64) sts.
Toe, all sizes: Toe Shaping chart (on Rnd 1 place markers where indicated). Total 60 sts.
Second side: Chart A 6 (7, 8) times. Total 48 (56, 64) sts.

Rnds 2 - 23 (24, 25):
First side: Chart A 6 (7, 8) times.
Toe, all sizes: Toe Shaping chart.
Second side: Chart A 6 (7, 8) times.

Total 108 (124, 140) sts remain.

Sole Toe - all sizes

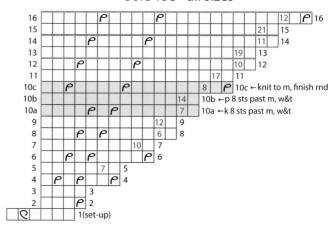

10c ← knit to m, finish rnd
10b ← p 8 sts past m, w&t
10a ← k 8 sts past m, w&t

Sole Heel - all sizes

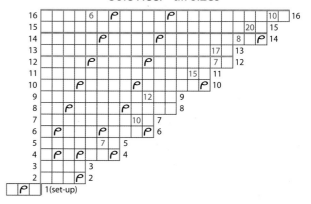

☐ k on RS, p on WS — end L
P M1F — end M
Q M1L — end S
☐ short row | center line
| BOR (beginning of round)

Chart notes:
Brown numbers give stitch counts greater than 5 to next symbol or end of chart.

After set-up round, work each row of chart twice; first from right to left, then from left to right.

OPTIONAL: When working from left to right, use M1B instead of M1F.

ZIP LINE

Rnd 24 (25, 26):

Work chart A 3 (4, 4) times, then work to * on Instep chart for your size.

Note: The * represents all sts in the zip line join; they do not appear individually on instep charts.

Join sides of lower foot: Drop working yarn and sl next 11 (14, 17) sts to RN. [If using circular needle(s), don't pull sts on RN to the cable yet.] Sl next 14 (17, 20) sts to dpn (temporary LN). Cut a separate strand of MC about 18" long. Leaving a 4" tail, work the first 3 sts on LN as follows: sl1 knitwise, sl 2tog knitwise, k3tog by inserting LN tfl of 3 sts on RN. Slip st just made back to LN without turning it. Then make a zip line up the foot with that separate strand by doing the following three steps 10 (13, 16) times:

1. sl 1 st from RN to LN
2. CDD with next 3 sts
3. sl st just made back to LN

Then do step 1 again, drop separate strand, pick up MC working yarn and do last zip CDD with it.

Finish round as follows: Continue to left side of Instep chart, then work chart A 3 (3,4) times. Total 84 (94, 104) sts remain.

Use a pin to mark center front stitch coming from zip line and position it as first st on LN. It will be the center of instep-shaping CDDs. See page 179 for handling a CDD that spans a needle intersection.

INSTEP

Rnds 25-43 (26-46, 27-49):

Work chart A 3 (4, 4) times, Instep chart for your size, and chart A 3 (3, 4) times. Total 56 (64, 72) sts remain.

ANKLE

Work chart A 7 (8, 9) times on each rnd until sock measures 5.5" (6", 6.5") [14cm (15cm, 16.5cm)] above sole.

LEG

Decide whether you need calf expansion (see page 179 for options). If not, work as for ankle for about 1.5" (2", 2.5") [4cm (5cm, 6.5cm)] or desired length. End having worked Rnd 1 or 5 of chart A.

Calf expansion by st increases: Work to end of Rnd 1 of chart A.

Rnds 1-32:

Work Calf Shaping chart from BOR, chart A 6 (7, 8) times, then work Calf Shaping chart to BOR. Total 72 (80, 88) sts.

End leg here or continue in pattern as established to length desired. End having worked Rnd 1 or 5 of chart A.

CUFF

Finish socks with cuff of your choice; see page 180 for options. Cuffs shown are 9 rnds of seed st followed by JSSBO (page 181), and 8 rnds of stockinette st bound off loosely, allowed to curl naturally to the front, then sewn down loosely.

FINISHING

Sew in yarn tails on WS, snugging up last st of zip line with tail hanging there.

> "
> A large oak tree is just a little nut that refused to give up.
>
> David McGee
> "

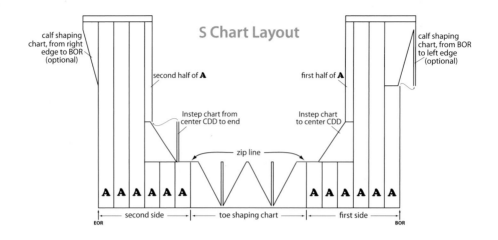

S Chart Layout

calf shaping chart, from right edge to BOR (optional)

second half of **A**

first half of **A**

calf shaping chart, from BOR to left edge (optional)

Instep chart from center CDD to end

Instep chart to center CDD

zip line

A A A A A A

A A A A A A

EOR

← second side →

← toe shaping chart →

← first side →

BOR

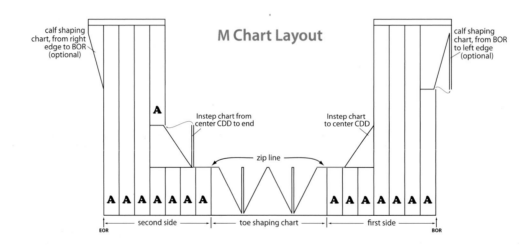

M Chart Layout

calf shaping chart, from right edge to BOR (optional)

calf shaping chart, from BOR to left edge (optional)

A

Instep chart from center CDD to end

Instep chart to center CDD

zip line

A A A A A A A

A A A A A A A

EOR

← second side →

← toe shaping chart →

← first side →

BOR

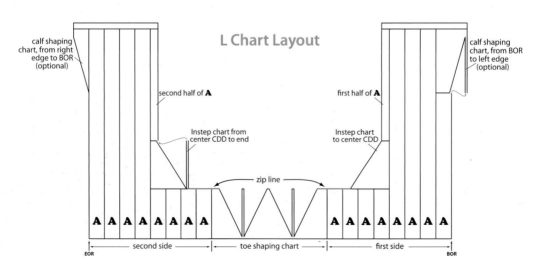

L Chart Layout

calf shaping chart, from right edge to BOR (optional)

calf shaping chart, from BOR to left edge (optional)

second half of **A**

first half of **A**

Instep chart from center CDD to end

Instep chart to center CDD

zip line

A A A A A A A A

A A A A A A A A

EOR

← second side →

← toe shaping chart →

← first side →

BOR

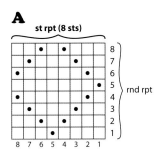

A

st rpt (8 sts)

knit — end L
• purl — end M
⋏ (any color) CDD — end S

Note: Use decrease symbols in black and color for your size only.
Treat as blank any squares which contain symbols for other sizes.

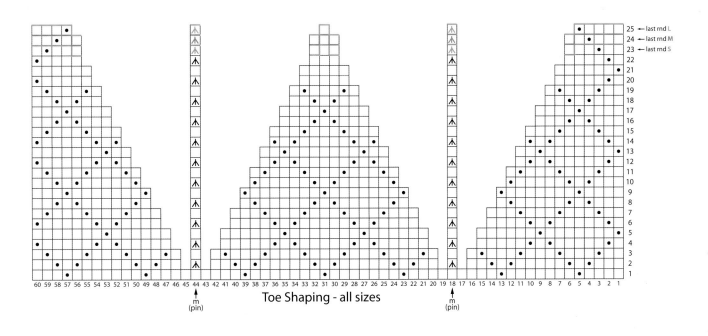

Toe Shaping - all sizes

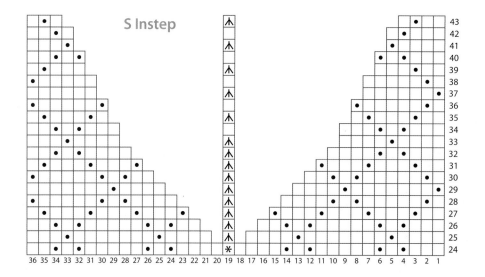

S Instep

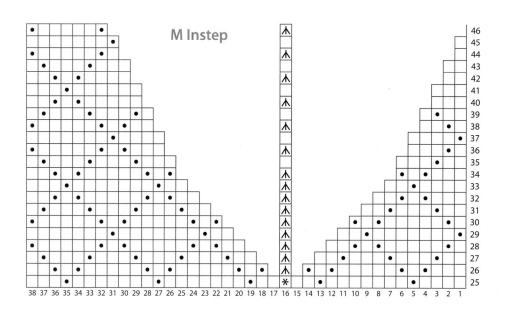

M Instep

☐ knit   ⋏ CDD   ⌿ M1F

• purl   ✳ see Zip Line in instructions   ⌐ M1B

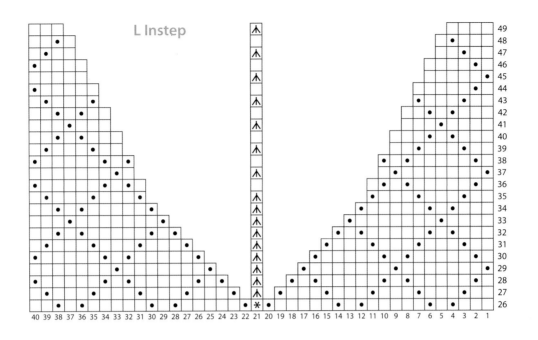

L Instep

Calf Shaping - all sizes

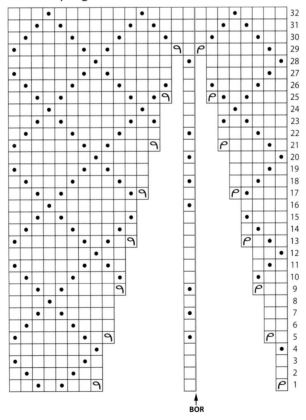

BOR

Syncopation

This "Galapagos" colorway of the Trekking Hand Art yarn called to me louder than all its neighbors on the shelf. I had to use it. It pairs beautifully with the semisolid half of the Handu Handdyed skein pair. The push and pull of the alternating blocks of stockinette stitch and linen stitch make the color stripes undulate and the cuff gently wave. And check out that cool curved zip line on the foot top!

Notes

- To prevent color blips from the old color showing up on the first row after a color change, there are no purls on the first round of the new color.
- It's your choice about whether to use a jog-handling technique (page 20) or not. The natural waviness of the stripes obscures the color jogs even without special treatment.
- The decreases or increases on the Instep and Calf Shaping charts force the omission of a few purls or slip stitches where they would normally occur in the stitch pattern. Don't worry; just follow the charts.

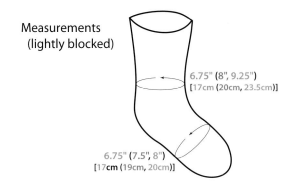

Measurements
(lightly blocked)

6.75" (8", 9.25")
[17cm (20cm, 23.5cm)]

6.75" (7.5", 8")
[17cm (19cm, 20cm)]

Yarn
Shown here:
- *Zitron Trekking Hand Art;* 75% New Wool / 25% nylon; 3.5 oz [100g], 459 yds [420 meters]; 1 (1, 1) skein Galapagos 514 (MC)
- *Handu Handdyed;* 75% wool / 25% polyamid; 1.75 oz [50g], 240 yds [220] meters; 1 (1, 1) skein in color way "Minty Fresh" semi-solid (CC)
- *Rowan Kidsilk Haze (optional reinforcement for sole);* 70% super kid mohair / 30% silk; 0.88 oz [25g], 230 yds [210 meters]; color 597; about 0.28 oz [8g] needed for women's medium

Needles
Change needle size if necessary to get gauge given.
- US size 1½ [2.5mm] — your choice: one long circular at least 40" [100cm], two shorter circulars, or dpns
- one dpn US size 1½ [2.5mm] — not needed if you're already using dpns
- US size 2 [2.75mm] for cuff in reverse linen st (optional) — your choice: one long circular at least 40" [100cm], two shorter circulars, or dpns

Notions
- stitch markers (2 pin-type, 4 any type in 3 colors: c1, c2, c3), tapestry needle

Gauge
- with reinforcing yarn on sole: 32 sts = 4" [10cm], 40 rnds = 4" [10cm]
- without reinforcing yarn, in pattern, unblocked: 36 sts = 4" [10cm], 60 rnds = 4" [10cm]

Size
small (S) - sole about 8.75" [22cm] long, for women's US shoe size 5-6 [Eur size 35/36]
medium (M) - sole about 9.5" [24cm] long, for women's US shoe size 7-8 [Eur size 37/38]
large (L) - sole about 10.25" [26cm] long, for women's US shoe size 9-10 [Eur size 39/40]

SOLE

Holding MC and reinforcement yarn (optional) together and using a variation of JMCO (page 181), cast on 46 (50, 54) pairs of sts on 2 needle points. Total 92 (100, 108) sts.

Rnd 1 (set-up):
Needle 1: K1, M1F, k1, pm c1 for end of heel, k41 (45, 49), pm c2 for beginning of toe, k3. Needle 2: K1, M1L, k1, pm c2 for end of toe, k41 (45, 49), pm c3 for beginning of heel and BOR (3 sts remain on LN after BOR marker). There are 6 heel sts, 6 toe sts, and 41 (45, 49) sts on each side. Total 94 (102, 110) sts.

Rnds 2 - 12 (14, 16):
Work Sole Heel chart between c3 and c1 markers, k41 (45, 49) side sts, work Sole Toe chart between c2 markers including SRs (page 184) as shown, and k41 (45, 49) side sts. Then k17 (20, 22) to center heel (new BOR for rest of sock). Total 154 (172, 190) sts.

Rnd 13 (15, 17):
Note: This round does not appear on Sole Toe and Sole Heel charts. Removing markers as you go, adjust st count for sock top as follows:
Size S: k15, k2tog, k120, k2tog, end k15.
Size M: k38, M1F, (k32, M1F) 3 times, end k38.
Size L: k23, M1F, (k 16, M1F) 9 times, end k23.

Cut reinforcing yarn. Total 152 (176, 200) sts.

FOOT

Toe Shaping

Refer to Chart Layout diagram for your size. From center heel BOR with CC, work as follows:

Rnd 1 (set-up):
First side: Work chart A 4 (5, 6) times. Total 48 (60, 72) sts.
Toe, all sizes: Work Toe Shaping chart (place markers where indicated). Total 56 sts.
Second side: Work chart A 4 (5, 6)) times. Total 48 (60, 72) sts.

Rnds 2 - 28 (29, 30):
First side: Work chart A 4 (5, 6) times.
Toe, all sizes: Work Toe Shaping chart.
Second side: Work chart A 4 (5, 6)) times.

Total 104 (128, 152) sts remain.

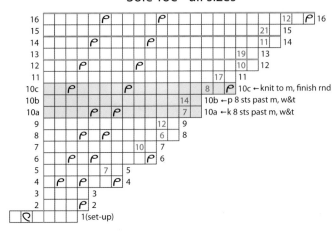

Sole Toe - all sizes

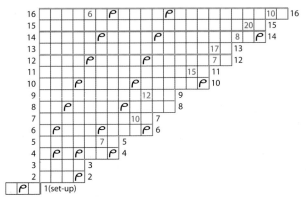

Sole Heel - all sizes

☐ k on RS, p on WS

℘ M1F

℧ M1L

☐ short row

— end L

— end M

— end S

| center line

| BOR (beginning of round)

Chart notes:

Brown numbers give stitch counts greater than 5 to next symbol or end of chart.

After set-up round, work each row of chart twice; first from right to left, then from left to right.

OPTIONAL: When working from left to right, use M1B instead of M1F.

ZIP LINE

Rnd 29 (30, 31):
Work chart A 2 (2, 3) times, then work to * on Instep chart for your size.
Note: The * represents all sts in the zip line join; they do not appear individually on instep charts.

Join sides of lower foot: Drop working yarn and sl next 12 (15, 18) sts to RN. [If using circular needle(s), don't pull sts on RN to the cable yet.] Sl next 14 (17, 20) sts to dpn (temporary LN). Cut a separate strand of CC about 18" long. Leaving a 4" tail, k2tog with the separate strand. Slip that st back to LN without turning it. Then make a zip line up the foot with that separate strand by doing the following three steps 11 (14, 17) times:
1. sl 1 st from RN to LN
2. CDD with next 3 sts
3. sl st just made back to LN

Then do step 1 again, drop the separate strand, pick up CC working yarn and do last zip CDD with it.

Finish rnd as follows: Continue to left side of Instep chart, then work chart A 2 (3, 3) times. Total 79 (97, 115) sts remain.

Use a pin to mark center front stitch coming from zip line and position it as first st on LN. It will be the center of instep-shaping CDDs. See page 179 for handling a CDD that spans a needle intersection.

INSTEP

Rnds 30-53 (31-57, 32-61):
Work chart A 2 (2, 3) times, Instep chart for your size, then chart A 2 (3, 3) times. Total 60 (72, 84) sts remain.

ANKLE

Continue as established — work chart A 5 (6, 7) times on each rnd — until sock measures 5.5" (6", 6.5") [14cm (15cm, 16.5cm)] above sole.

LEG

Decide whether you need calf expansion (see page 179 for options). If not, work as for ankle for about 1.5" (2", 2.5") [4cm (5cm, 6.5cm)] or desired length. End having worked Rnd 11 of chart A (first rnd of MC stripe).

Calf expansion by st increases: Work to end of Rnd 10 of chart A (last rnd of CC stripe).

Rnds 1-41:
Work Calf Shaping chart from BOR, chart A 3 (4, 5) times, then Calf Shaping chart to BOR. Total 72 (84, 96) sts.

End leg here or continue in pattern as established to length desired. End having worked Rnd 11 of chart A (first rnd of MC stripe).

CUFF

Finish socks with cuff of your choice in MC; see page 180 for options. One cuff shown is 4-st cord BO. The other is 6 rnds of reverse linen st using 2 strands of MC, then bound off in knit.

FINISHING

Sew in yarn tails on WS, snugging up last st of zip line with tail hanging there.

> "
> The chief danger in life
> is that you may take too
> many precautions.
>
> Alfred Adler
>
> "

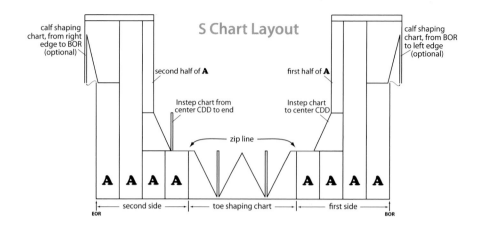

S Chart Layout

calf shaping chart, from right edge to BOR (optional)

second half of **A**

Instep chart from center CDD to end

zip line

first half of **A**

Instep chart to center CDD

calf shaping chart, from BOR to left edge (optional)

A A A A   **A A A A**

EOR ⊢—— second side ——⊣ ⊢—— toe shaping chart ——⊣ ⊢—— first side ——⊣ BOR

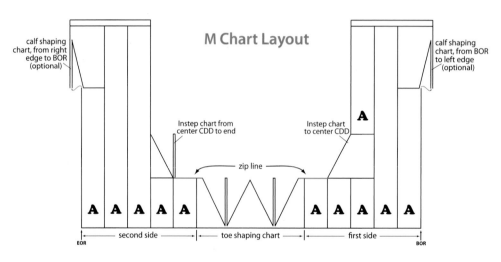

M Chart Layout

calf shaping chart, from right edge to BOR (optional)

Instep chart from center CDD to end

zip line

Instep chart to center CDD

A

calf shaping chart, from BOR to left edge (optional)

A A A A A   **A A A A A**

EOR ⊢—— second side ——⊣ ⊢—— toe shaping chart ——⊣ ⊢—— first side ——⊣ BOR

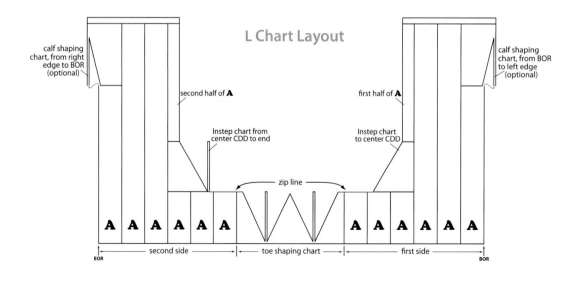

L Chart Layout

calf shaping chart, from right edge to BOR (optional)

second half of **A**

Instep chart from center CDD to end

zip line

first half of **A**

Instep chart to center CDD

calf shaping chart, from BOR to left edge (optional)

A A A A A A   **A A A A A A**

EOR ⊢—— second side ——⊣ ⊢—— toe shaping chart ——⊣ ⊢—— first side ——⊣ BOR

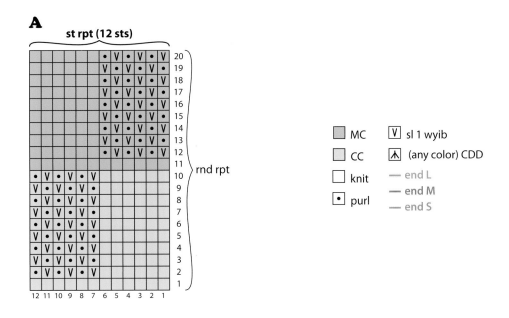

A

st rpt (12 sts)

MC   **V** sl 1 wyib

CC   **⅄** (any color) CDD

knit   — end L

• purl   — end M

    — end S

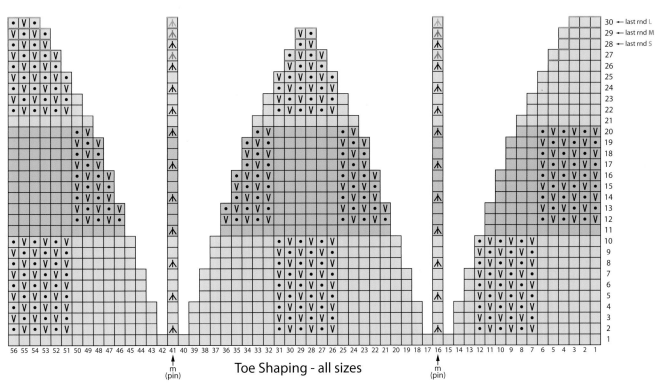

Toe Shaping - all sizes

Note: Use decrease symbols in black and color for your size only.
Treat as blank any squares which contain symbols for other sizes.

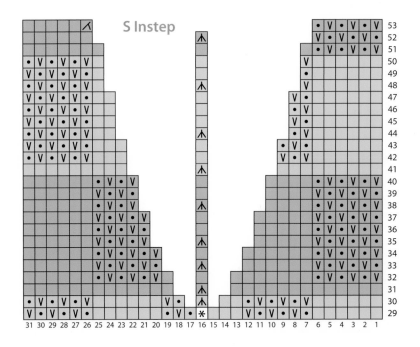

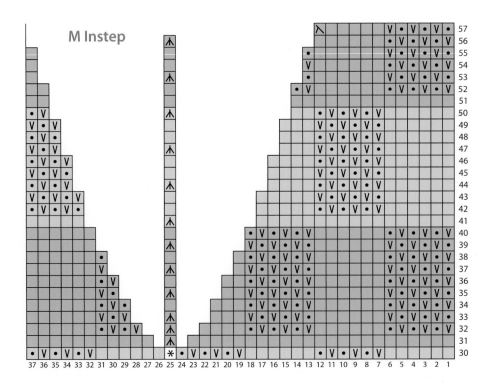

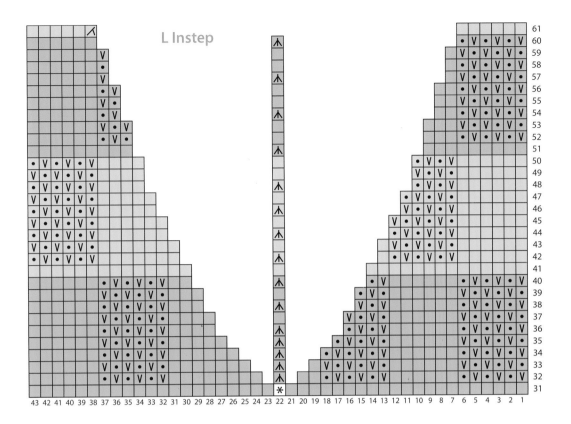

L Instep

MC   sl 1 wyib [V]

CC   CDD [⋏]

knit   k2tog [╱]

purl [•]   ssk [╲]

[✱] see Zip Line in instructions

Calf Shaping - all sizes

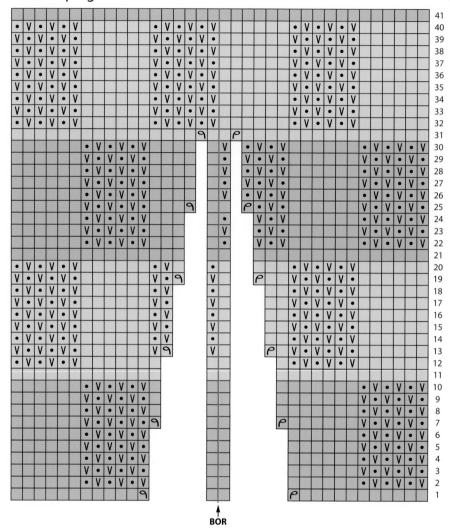

MC · V sl 1 wyib

CC · M1F

knit · M1B

purl

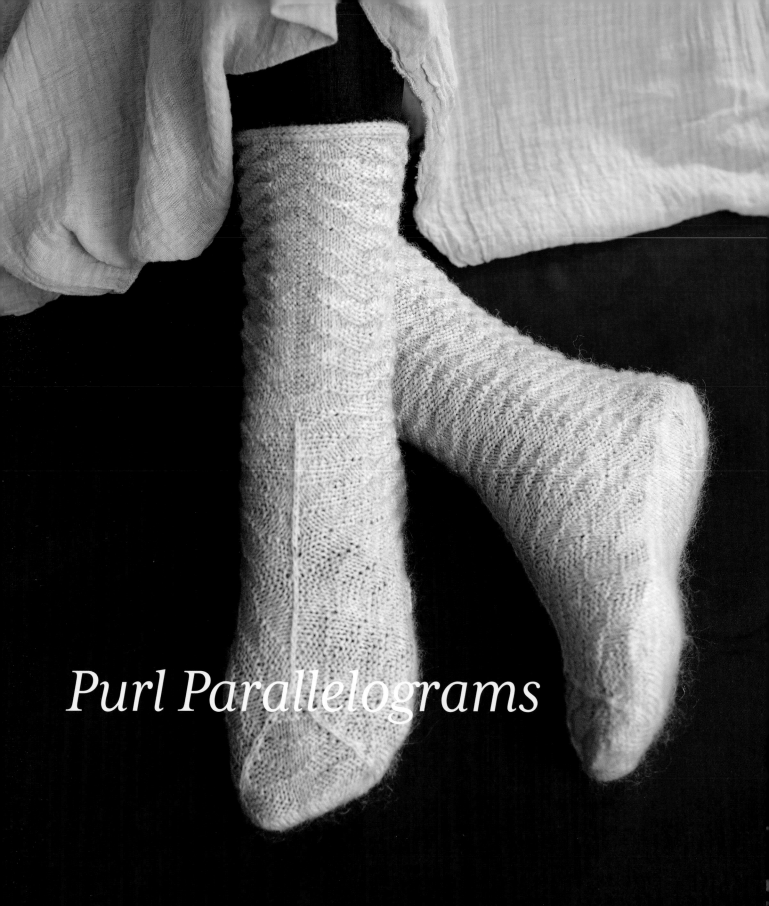

Purl Parallelograms

I thought this pattern stitch would read diagonally because all the parallelograms lean markedly toward the center front. Instead, soft vertical peaks and valleys formed. Areas of knit stitches stack on top of each other making peaks, and purl areas do the same to form valleys. Serendipitously, that gives this sock a little extra elasticity.

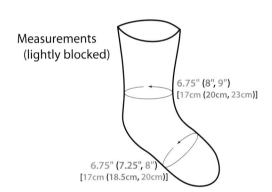

Measurements
(lightly blocked)

6.75" (8", 9")
[17cm (20cm, 23cm)]

6.75" (7.25", 8")
[17cm (18.5cm, 20cm)]

Note
● Because the left and right sides of each sock mirror each other, the parallelograms morph into other symmetrical shapes at the toe decrease lines and the center front and back. Have fun finding triangles, chevrons, isosceles trapezoids, and other forms in those areas.

Yarn
Shown here:
● *Regia 4-Fach Haltbar;* 75% Superwash New Wool / 25% Polyamid; 1.75 oz [50g], 230 yds [210 meters]; 2 (2, 3) balls color 02143(MC)
● *Rowan Kidsilk Haze (optional reinforcement for sole);* 70% super kid mohair / 30% silk; 0.88 oz [25g], 229 yds [210 meters]; color 634; about 0.28 oz [8g] needed for women's medium

Needles
Change needle size if necessary to get the gauge given.
● US size 1½ [2.5mm] for sole with reinforcing yarn — your choice: one long circular at least 40" [100cm], two shorter circulars, or dpns
● US size 1 [2.25mm] for sock top — your choice: one long circular at least 40" [100cm], two shorter circulars, or dpns
● one dpn US size 1 [2.25mm] — not needed if you're already using dpns

Notions
● stitch markers (2 pin-type, 4 any type in 3 colors: c1, c2, c3), tapestry needle

Gauge
● with reinforcing yarn on sole: 32 sts = 4" [10cm], 40 rnds = 4" [10cm]
● without reinforcing yarn, in pattern, unblocked: 35 sts = 4" [10cm], 54 rnds = 4" [10cm]

Size
small (S) - sole about 8.75" [22cm] long, for women's US shoe size 5-6 [Eur size 35/36]
medium (M) - sole about 9.5" [24cm] long, for women's US shoe size 7-8 [Eur size 37/38]
large (L) - sole about 10.25" [26cm] long, for women's US shoe size 9-10 [Eur size 39/40]

SOLE

Holding MC and reinforcement yarn (optional) together and using a variation of JMCO (page 181), cast on 46 (50, 54) pairs of sts on 2 needle points. Total 92 (100, 108) sts.

Rnd 1 (set-up):
Needle 1: K1, M1F, k1, pm c1 for end of heel, k41 (45, 49), pm c2 for beginning of toe, k3. Needle 2: K1, M1L, k1, pm c2 for end of toe, k41 (45, 49), pm c3 for beginning of heel and BOR (3 sts remain on LN after BOR marker). There are 6 heel sts, 6 toe sts, and 41 (45, 49) sts on each side. Total 94 (102, 110) sts.

Rnds 2 - 12 (14, 16):
Work Sole Heel chart between c3 and c1 markers, k41 (45, 49) side sts, work Sole Toe chart between c2 markers including SRs (page 184) as shown, and k41 (45, 49) side sts. Then k17 (20, 22) to center heel (new BOR for rest of sock). Total 154 (172, 190) sts.

Rnd 13 (15, 17):
Note: This round does not appear on Sole Toe and Sole Heel charts.

Removing markers as you go, adjust st count for sock top as follows:
Size S: k10, k2tog, k20, k2tog, k86, k2tog, k20, k2tog, end k10.
Size M: k15, k2tog, k138, k2tog, end k15.
Size L: Knit.

Cut reinforcing yarn. Total 150 (170, 190) sts.

FOOT

Toe Shaping

Refer to Chart Layout diagram for your size. From center heel BOR with 2.25mm needle, work as follows:

Rnd 1 (set-up):
First side: Work chart A 5 (6, 7) times. Total 50 (60, 70) sts.
Toe, all sizes: Work Toe Shaping chart (place markers where indicated). Total 50 sts.
Second side: Work chart B 5 (6, 7) times. Total 50 (60, 70) sts.

Rnds 2 - 23 (24, 25):
First side: Work chart A 5 (6, 7) times.
Toe, all sizes: Work Toe Shaping chart.
Second side: Work chart B 5 (6, 7) times.

Total 102 (122, 142) sts remain.

Sole Toe - all sizes

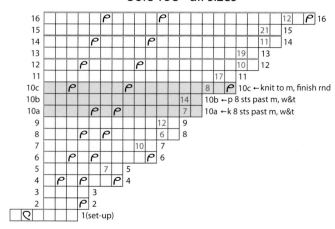

Sole Heel - all sizes

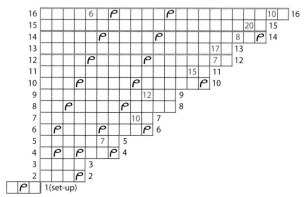

Chart notes:

Brown numbers give stitch counts greater than 5 to next symbol or end of chart.

After set-up round, work each row of chart twice; first from right to left, then from left to right.

OPTIONAL: When working from left to right, use M1B instead of M1F.

Legend:
- ☐ k on RS, p on WS
- ℗ M1F
- ℧ M1L
- ▨ short row
- — end L
- — end M
- — end S
- | center line
- ▐ **BOR** (beginning of round)

ZIP LINE

Rnd 24 (25, 26):
Work chart A 2 (3, 3) times, then work to * on Instep chart for your size.

Note: The * represents all sts in the zip line join; they do not appear individually on instep charts.

Join sides of lower foot: Drop working yarn and sl next 11 (14, 17) sts to RN. [If using circular needle(s), don't pull sts on RN to the cable yet.] Sl next 13 (16, 19) to dpn (temporary LN). Cut a separate strand of MC about 18" long. Leaving a 4" tail, k2tog with the separate strand of yarn. Slip that st back to LN without turning it. Then make a zip line up the foot with that separate strand by doing the following three steps 10 (13, 16) times:
1. sl 1 st from RN to LN
2. CDD with next 3 sts
3. sl st just made back to LN

Then do step 1 again, drop the separate strand, pick up MC working yarn and do last zip CDD with it.

Finish round as follows: Continue to left side of Instep chart, then work chart B 3 (3, 4) times. Total 79 (93, 107) sts remain.

Use a pin to mark center front stitch coming from zip line and position it as first st on LN. It will be the center of instep-shaping CDDs. See page 179 for handling a CDD that spans a needle intersection.

INSTEP

Rnds 25-44 (26-46, 27-48):
Work chart A 2 (3, 3) times, Instep chart for your size, then chart B 3 (3, 4) times. Total 60 (70, 80) sts remain.

ANKLE

Work charts as follows for each rnd until sock measures 5.5" (6", 6.5") [14cm (15cm, 16.5cm)] above sole:
Sizes S & L: Chart A 3 (4) times and chart B 3 (4) times.
Size M: Chart A 3 times, chart A to line C, chart B from line D, and chart B 3 times.

LEG

Decide whether you need calf expansion (see page 179 for options). If not, work as for ankle for about 1.5" (2", 2.5") [4cm (5cm, 6.5cm)] or desired length. End having worked Rnd 6 of charts A and B.

Calf expansion by st increases: Work to end of Rnd 6 of charts A and B.

Sizes S & L Rnds 1-18:
Work Calf Shaping chart from BOR, chart A 2 (3) times, chart B 2 (3) times, then Calf Shaping chart to BOR. Total 70 (90) sts.

Size M Rnds 1-18:
Work Calf Shaping chart from BOR, chart A 2 times, chart A to line C, chart B from line D, and chart B 2 times, then Calf Shaping chart to BOR. Total 80 sts.

End leg here or continue in pattern as established to length desired. End having worked Rnd 6 of charts A and B.

CUFF

Finish socks with cuff of your choice; see page 180 for options. Cuffs shown are 4-st cord BO.

FINISHING

Sew in yarn tails on WS, snugging up last st of zip line with tail hanging there.

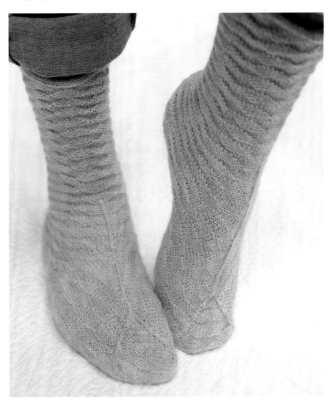

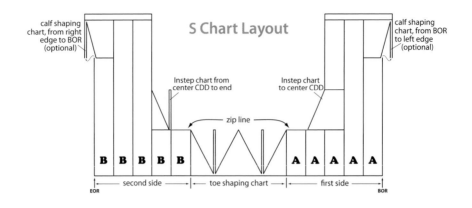

S Chart Layout

calf shaping chart, from right edge to BOR (optional)

calf shaping chart, from BOR to left edge (optional)

Instep chart from center CDD to end

Instep chart to center CDD

zip line

B B B B B   A A A A A

EOR — second side — toe shaping chart — first side — BOR

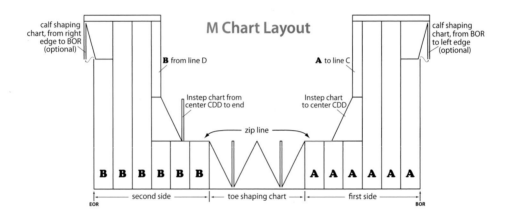

M Chart Layout

calf shaping chart, from right edge to BOR (optional)

calf shaping chart, from BOR to left edge (optional)

B from line D

A to line C

Instep chart from center CDD to end

Instep chart to center CDD

zip line

B B B B B B   A A A A A A

EOR — second side — toe shaping chart — first side — BOR

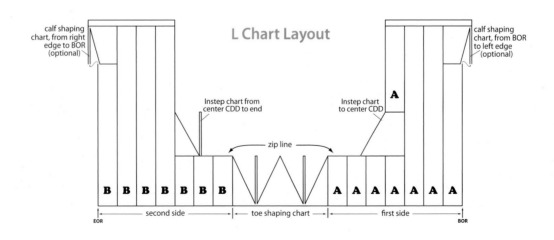

L Chart Layout

calf shaping chart, from right edge to BOR (optional)

calf shaping chart, from BOR to left edge (optional)

Instep chart from center CDD to end

Instep chart to center CDD

A

zip line

B B B B B B B   A A A A A A A

EOR — second side — toe shaping chart — first side — BOR

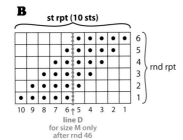

B st rpt (10 sts)

rnd rpt

10 9 8 7 6 ↑ 5 4 3 2 1

line D
for size M only
after rnd 46

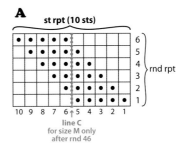

A st rpt (10 sts)

rnd rpt

10 9 8 7 6 ↑ 5 4 3 2 1

line C
for size M only
after rnd 46

☐ knit   — end L

▣ purl   — end M

⩓ (any color) CDD   — end S

Note: Use decrease symbols in black and color for your size only.
Treat as blank any squares which contain symbols for other sizes.

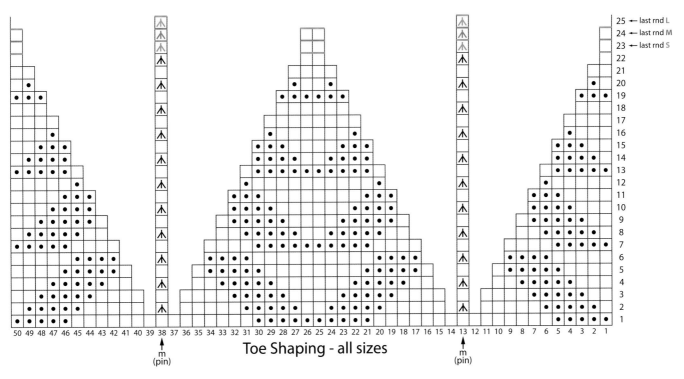

Toe Shaping - all sizes

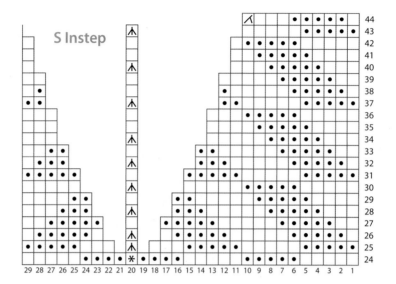

S Instep

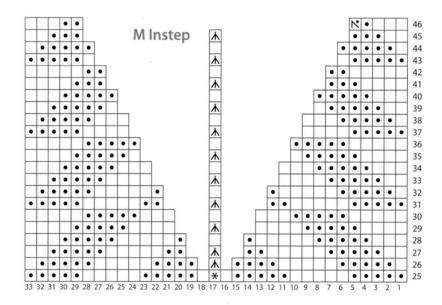

M Instep

> "
> It does not matter how
> slowly you go as long as
> you do not stop.
>
> Confucius
> "

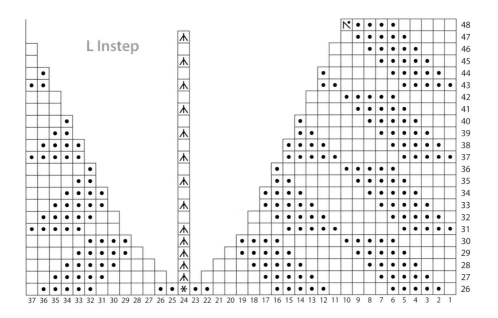

L Instep

knit		p2tog		M1F
purl		CDD		M1B
k2tog		see Zip Line in instructions		

Calf Shaping - all sizes

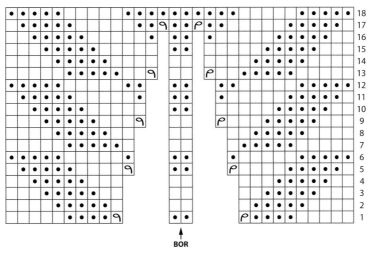

BOR

Irises

The yarn itself inspired this impressionistic design. It is Handu Handdyed and comes in two 50-gram color-coordinated skeins, one solid and one variegated. The colorway is called "Iris," and for me it evoked memories of iris beds in glorious colors. I found two more solid yarns in iris colors and put them all together in an easy slip-stitch pattern that only looks complicated. Every other color stripe blends into the color stripe above it via slip stitches, and the variegated skein of Handu keeps the results from looking too uniform.

Notes:

- This design is very busy, so I minimized the visual effect of the toe- and instep-shaping lines by substituting paired single decreases (ssk and k2tog) for the centered double decreases.
- The stitch pattern contracts vertically because of stitches being slipped on two consecutive rounds; that's why the total number of rounds in the sock top is surprisingly greater than you might expect.
- Even though this sock is worked in horizontal color stripes, the slip-stitch pattern completely obscures the color jog. No special jog-handling method is needed until you come to the cuff. Because the cuff is worked in one of the contrasting colors, you may opt to give the jog special treatment (see page 20) on just that one transition round.

Yarn

Shown here:
- **Madelinetosh Tosh Sock;** 100% superwash merino wool; 3.5 oz [100g], 395 yds [361 meters]; 1 (1, 1) skein "Ms. Taylor" (MC)
- **Handu Handdyed;** 75% wool / 25% polyamid; each skein is 1.75 oz [50g], 240 yds [220 meters]; 1 (1, 1) set of 2 skeins in colorway "Iris" variegated (CC1) and solid (CC2)
- **Stitchjones Titanium Sock;** 75% superwash merino / 25% nylon; 3.5 oz [100g], 425 yds [389 meters]; 1 (1, 1) skein "Royal Plum" (CC3)
- **Schulana Kid Seta (optional reinforcement for sole);** 70% super kid mohair / 30% silk; 0.88 oz [25g], 230 yds [210 meters]; color 22; about 0.28 oz [8g] needed for women's medium

Needles

Change needle size if necessary to get gauge given.
- US size 1½ [2.5mm] — your choice: one long circular at least 40" [100cm], two shorter circulars, or dpns
- one dpn US size 1½ [2.5mm] — not needed if you're already using dpns

Notions

- stitch markers (2 pin-type, 4 any type in 3 colors: c1, c2, c3), tapestry needle

Gauge

- with reinforcing yarn on sole: 32 sts = 4" [10cm], 40 rnds = 4" [10cm]
- without reinforcing yarn, in pattern, unblocked: 34 sts = 4" [10cm], 64 rnds = 4" [10cm]

Size

small (S) - sole about 8.75" [22cm] long, for women's US shoe size 5-6 [Eur size 35/36]

medium (M) - sole about 9.5" [24cm] long, for women's US shoe size 7-8 [Eur size 37/38]

large (L) - sole about 10.25" [26cm] long, for women's US shoe size 9-10 [Eur size 39/40]

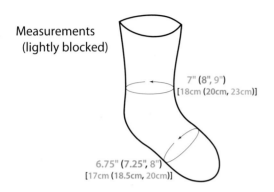

Measurements
(lightly blocked)

7" (8", 9")
[18cm (20cm, 23cm)]

6.75" (7.25", 8")
[17cm (18.5cm, 20cm)]

Sole Toe - all sizes

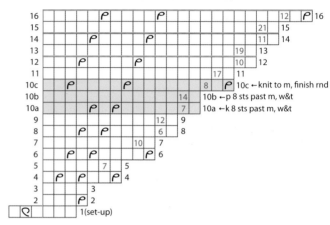

10c ←knit to m, finish rnd
10b ←p 8 sts past m, w&t
10a ←k 8 sts past m, w&t

Sole Heel - all sizes

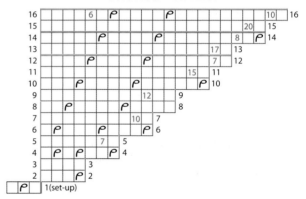

SOLE

Holding MC and reinforcement yarn (optional) together and using a variation of JMCO (page 181), cast on 46 (50, 54) pairs of sts on 2 needle points. Total 92 (100, 108) sts.

Rnd 1 (set-up):

Needle 1: K1, M1F, k1, pm c1 for end of heel, k41 (45, 49), pm c2 for beginning of toe, k3. Needle 2: K1, M1L, k1, pm c2 for end of toe, k41 (45, 49), pm c3 for beginning of heel and BOR (3 sts remain on LN after BOR marker). There are 6 heel sts, 6 toe sts, and 41 (45, 49) sts on each side. Total 94 (102, 110) sts.

Rnds 2 - 12 (14, 16):

Work Sole Heel chart between c3 and c1 markers, k41 (45, 49) side sts, work Sole Toe chart between c2 markers including SRs (page 184) as shown, and k41 (45, 49) side sts. Then k17 (20, 22) to center heel (new BOR for rest of sock). Total 154 (172, 190) sts.

Rnd 13 (15, 17):

Note: This round does not appear on Sole Toe and Sole Heel charts.

Removing markers as you go, adjust st count for sock top as follows:

Size S: k50, M1F, k54, M1F, end k50.
Size M: Knit.
Size L: k60, M1F, k70, M1F, end k60.

Cut reinforcing yarn. Total 156 (172, 192) sts.

Chart notes:

Brown numbers give stitch counts greater than 5 to next symbol or end of chart.

After set-up round, work each row of chart twice; first from right to left, then from left to right.

OPTIONAL: When working from left to right, use M1B instead of M1F.

Legend:
- ☐ k on RS, p on WS
- 𝒫 M1F
- ℛ M1L
- ▨ short row
- — end L
- — end M
- — end S
- │ center line
- │ **BOR** (beginning of round)

FOOT
Toe Shaping

Refer to Chart Layout diagram. From center heel BOR with CC2, work as follows:

Rnd 1 (set-up):
First side: Work chart A 27 (31, 36) times. Total 54 (62, 72) sts.
Toe, all sizes: Work Toe Shaping chart (place markers where indicated). Total 48sts.
Second side: Work chart A 27 (31, 36) times. Total 54 (62, 72) sts.

Rnds 2 - 27 (28, 29):
First side: Work chart A 27 (31, 36) times.
Toe, all sizes: Work Toe Shaping chart.
Second side: Work chart A 27 (31, 36) times.

Total 112 (128, 148) sts remain.

GRAFTED FOOT JOIN
Rnd 28 (29, 30):

Work chart A 14 (16, 18) times, then work to * on Instep chart for your size.

Note: The * represents all sts in the grafted join; they do not appear individually on instep charts.

Join sides of lower foot: Drop working yarn and sl next 14 (17, 21) sts to RN. [If using circular needle(s), don't pull sts on RN to the cable yet.] Cut a separate strand of yarn about 18" long in same color as the rnd you're working and thread it in the tapestry needle. Leaving a 4" tail and working from toe end with separate strand, graft (Kitchener stitch) the first 14 (17, 21) sts on RN and LN together (page 181). With the separate strand, M1F on LN.

Finish rnd as follows: Pick up working yarn and knit st just made. Work to left side of Instep chart, then work chart A 14 (16, 18) times. Total 85 (95, 107) sts remain.

Note: the M1F will be loose until neatened during finishing.

Use a pin to mark center front stitch, the one coming from the M1F, and position it as first st on LN. It will be the stitch between the pairs of ssk and K2tog decreases which shape the instep.

INSTEP

Rnds 29-50 (30-54, 31-58):

Work chart A 14 (16, 18) times, Instep chart for your size, then chart A 14 (16, 18) times. Total 60 (68, 76) sts remain.

ANKLE

Work chart A 30 (34, 38) times for each rnd. End having worked Rnd 80 (88, 96).

LEG

Decide whether you need calf expansion (see page 179 for options). If not, work as for ankle through Rnd 117 (127, 137) or any MC rnd.

Calf expansion by st increases
Rnds 81 (89, 97) - 112 (120, 128):

Work from BOR of Calf Shaping chart to left side, chart A 28 (32, 36) times, then Calf Shaping chart to BOR. Continue in pattern as established through Rnd 117 (127, 137)) or to length desired. End having worked an MC rnd. Total 72 (80, 88) sts.

CUFF

Finish socks with cuff of your choice in MC; see page 180 for options. Cuffs shown are 4-st cord BO and faced border with picot edge.

Faced border with picot edge:
Rnds 1 - 6: Knit.
Rnd 7: *YO, k2tog*, repeat to end of rnd.
Rnd 8: Knit.
Rnd 9: k3, k2tog, (k6, k2tog) as many times as will fit in the rnd, knit to end of rnd.
Rnds 10 - 12: Knit.
Bind off loosely, sew facing down on WS.

FINISHING

Sew in yarn tails on WS, snugging up last st of foot join graft with tail hanging there.

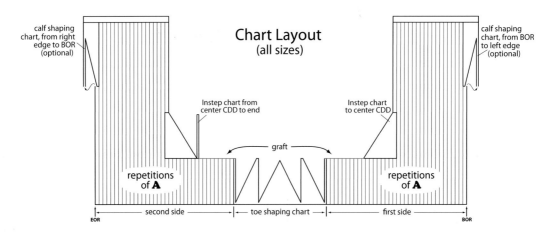

Chart Layout
(all sizes)

calf shaping chart, from right edge to BOR (optional)

calf shaping chart, from BOR to left edge (optional)

Instep chart from center CDD to end

Instep chart to center CDD

graft

repetitions of **A**

repetitions of **A**

| EOR | second side | toe shaping chart | first side | BOR |

A

st rpt

		40	80	120	
	V	39	79	119	
		38	78	118	
		37	77	117	
V		36	76	116	
V		35	75	115	
		34	74	114	
		33	73	113	
	V	32	72	112	
	V	31	71	111	
		30	70	110	
		29	69	109	
V		28	68	108	
V		27	67	107	
		26	66	106	
		25	65	105	
	V	24	64	104	
	V	23	63	103	
		22	62	102	
		21	61	101	
V		20	60	100	
V		19	59	99	
		18	58	98	
		17	57	97	137
	V	16	56	96	136
	V	15	55	95	135
		14	54	94	134
		13	53	93	133
V		12	52	92	132
V		11	51	91	131
		10	50	90	130
		9	49	89	129
	V	8	48	88	128
	V	7	47	87	127
		6	46	86	126
		5	45	85	125
V		4	44	84	124
V		3	43	83	123
		2	42	82	122
		1	41	81	121

2   1

> **"**
>
> Creativity is allowing yourself to make mistakes; art is knowing which ones to keep.
>
> Scott Adams
>
> **"**

Note: Use decrease symbols in black and color for your size only.
Treat as blank any squares which contain symbols for other sizes.

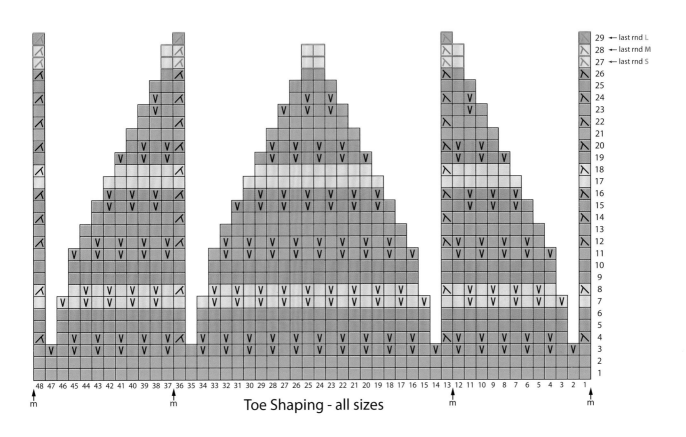

Toe Shaping - all sizes

	MC		knit	— end L
	CC1	V	sl 1 wyib	— end M
	CC2	⅄	(any color) ssk	— end S
	CC3	⋌	(any color) k2tog	

Calf Shaping - all sizes

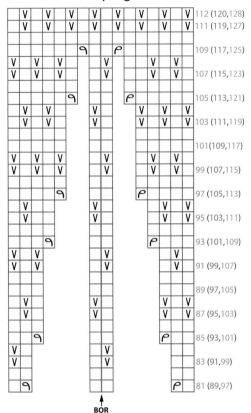

112 (120,128)
111 (119,127)
109 (117,125)
107 (115,123)
105 (113,121)
103 (111,119)
101(109,117)
99 (107,115)
97 (105,113)
95 (103,111)
93 (101,109)
91 (99,107)
89 (97,105)
87 (95,103)
85 (93,101)
83 (91,99)
81 (89,97)

BOR

▨ MC	☐ (any color) knit
▨ CC1	Ⅴ sl 1 wyib
▨ CC2	◺ ssk ℙ M1F
▨ CC3	◿ k2tog ৭ M1B
✳ see Grafted Foot Join in instructions	

Match round numbers for your size to round numbers on chart A to determine yarn color for each calf shaping round.

S Instep

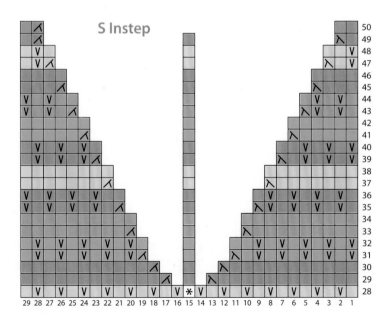

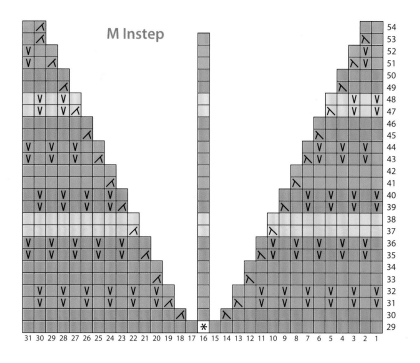

M Instep

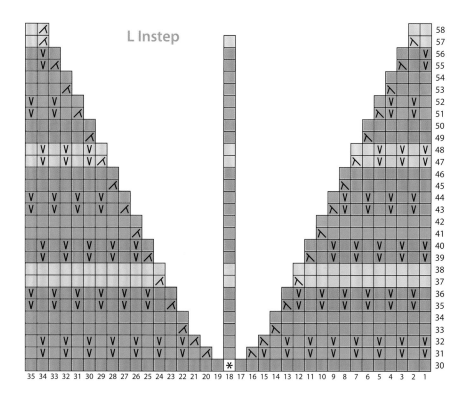

L Instep

INCREASING AND DECREASING

Balanced Biases

Biased diagonal panels, formed by increasing on one side and decreasing on the other, are an interesting way to break up the horizontal lines formed by variegated yarn. Before I knit this, I thought the variegated color lines would form zigzags. Instead, they climbed stairs and even pushed the center back up a little. I really like that, even though I still don't know exactly why it happened.

I did figure out why the bias panels have more stitches per inch than the vertical sections: it's because the diagonal of a rectangle (such as a stockinette stitch) is longer than its longest side. The same geometric law causes the bias panels to need more rounds per inch than the vertical ones. That means the bias panels have to be lengthened every eighth round by short rows. I used a subtle contrasting color for those rounds, thus emphasizing those intriguing stair steps and providing a little structure to the color variegation.

Notes

- The design principle is simple here — six-stitch bias panels symmetrically converging and diverging — but converting that to charts and instructions for three sizes makes the process seem complicated. Keeping the design principle in mind will help. Even so, this sock pattern probably qualifies as challenging.
- The reason some decreases have to be displaced on bias panels close to the instep shaping is to keep the stitch count constant while maintaining stitch-pattern integrity. No worries; just follow the charts.
- Work all wraps as they are encountered on the stitches directly above the wrap-and-turn (w&t) symbols on the charts.

Yarn

Shown here:
- Blue Moon Socks that Rock; 100% superwash merino - mediumweight; 5.5 oz [156g], 380 yds [347 meters]; 1 (1, 1) skein Ms. LaRock (MC)
- Blue Moon Socks that Rock; 100% superwash merino - mediumweight; 5.5 oz [156g], 380 yds [347 meters]; 1 (1, 1) skein Spinel (CC)
- (note: no reinforcement yarn used on soles of sample socks because yarn is relatively thick)

Needles

Change needle size if necessary to get gauge given.
- US size 1½ [2.5mm] — your choice: one long circular at least 40" [100cm], two shorter circulars, or dpns
- one dpn US size 1½ [2.5mm] — not needed if you're already using dpns

Notions

- stitch markers (2 pin-type, 4 any type in 3 colors: c1, c2, c3), tapestry needle

Gauge

- in stockinette stitch with no reinforcing yarn (sole): 28 sts = 4" [10cm], 40 rnds = 4" [10cm]
- in pattern, unblocked: 31 sts = 4" [10cm], 40 rnds = 4" [10cm]

Size

small (S) - sole about 8.75" [22cm] long, for women's US shoe size 5-6 [Eur size 35/36]
medium (M) - sole about 9.5" [24cm] long, for women's US shoe size 7-8 [Eur size 37/38]
large (L) - sole about 10.25" [26cm] long, for women's US shoe size 9-10 [Eur size 39/40]

Sole Toe - all sizes

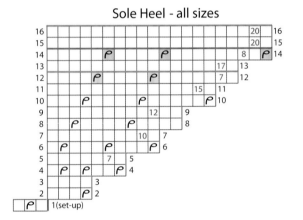

10c ←knit to m, finish rnd
10b ←p 8 sts past m, w&t
10a ←k 8 sts past m, w&t

1 (set-up)

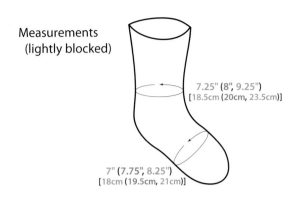

**Measurements
(lightly blocked)**

7.25" (8", 9.25")
[18.5cm (20cm, 23.5cm)]

7" (7.75", 8.25")
[18cm (19.5cm, 21cm)]

SOLE

Using CC and a variation of JMCO (page 181), cast on 39 (42, 46) pairs of sts on 2 needle points. Total 78 (84, 92) sts.

Rnd 1 (set-up):
Needle 1: K1, M1F, k1, pm c1 for end of heel, k34 (37, 41), pm c2 for beginning of toe, k3. Needle 2: K1, M1L, k1, pm c2 for end of toe, k34 (37, 41), pm c3 for beginning of heel and BOR (3 sts remain on LN after BOR marker). There are 6 heel sts, 6 toe sts, and 34 (37, 41) sts on each side. Total 80 (86, 94) sts.

Rnds 2 - 12 (14, 16):
Work Sole Heel chart between c3 and c1 markers, k34 (37, 41) side sts, work Sole Toe chart between c2 markers including SRs (page 184) as shown, and k34 (37, 41) side sts. Then k15 (17, 20) to center heel (new BOR for rest of sock). Total 132 (146, 164) sts.

Rnd 13 (15, 17):
Note: This round does not appear on Sole Toe and Sole Heel charts. Removing markers as you go, adjust st count for sock top as follows: k13 (18, 17), k2tog, [k24 (52, 30), k2tog] 4 (2, 4) times, end k13 (18, 17). Total 127 (143, 159) sts.

FOOT
Toe Shaping

Refer to Chart Layout diagram for your size. From center heel BOR with MC, work the charts for your size as follows:

Rnd 1 (set-up):
First side: Work chart A, then st rpt of chart A 1 (2, 2) times. In addition for sizes S and L, work the 8 sts from beginning of st rpt to line E. Total 44 (52, 60) sts.

Sole Heel - all sizes

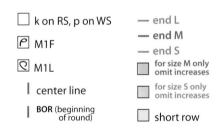

1 (set-up)

Chart notes:

Brown numbers give stitch counts greater than 5 to next symbol or end of chart.

After set-up round, work each row of chart twice; first from right to left, then from left to right.

OPTIONAL: When working from left to right, use M1B instead of M1F.

Legend:
- ☐ k on RS, p on WS
- ℘ M1F
- ℞ M1L
- | center line
- ❘ BOR (beginning of round)
- — end L
- — end M
- — end S
- ▨ for size M only omit increases
- ▨ for size S only omit increases
- ☐ short row

Toe, all sizes: Work Toe Shaping chart (place markers where indicated). Total 40 sts.
Second side: Work chart B from line F (beginning, line F) to end of st rpt, st rpt 1 (1, 2) times, then full chart B. Total 43 (51, 59) sts.

Rnds 2 - 20 (21, 22):
First side: Work chart A, then chart A st rpt 1 (2, 2) times. In addition for sizes S and L, work the 8 sts from beginning of st rpt to line E.
Toe, all sizes: Work Toe Shaping chart.
Second side: Work chart B from line F (beginning, line F) to end of st rpt, st rpt 1 (1, 2) times, then full chart B. Total 91 (107, 123) sts remain.

GRAFTED FOOT JOIN

Rnd 21 (22, 23):
Work full chart A, then chart A st rpt to line E (line C, end of st rpt). Work to * on Instep chart for your size.
Note: The * represents all sts in the grafted join; they do not appear individually on instep charts.

Join sides of lower foot: Drop working yarn and sl next 9 (11, 13) sts to RN. [If using circular needle(s), don't pull sts on RN to the cable yet.] Cut a separate strand of MC about 18" long and thread it in the tapestry needle. Leaving a 4" tail and working from toe end with separate strand, graft (Kitchener stitch) the first 9 (11, 13) sts on RN and LN together (page 181). With separate strand, M1F on LN.

Finish rnd as follows: Pick up working yarn and knit st just made. Work to left side of Instep chart, work chart B from line F (line D, beg of st rpt) to end of st rpt, then full chart B. Total 74 (86, 98) sts remain.
Note: the M1F st will be loose until neatened during finishing.

Use a pin to mark center front stitch, the one coming from the M1F, and position it as first st on LN. It will be the center of instep-shaping CDDs. See page 179 for handling a CDD that spans a needle intersection.

INSTEP

Rnds 22-37 (23-40, 24-43):
Using charts for your size, work full chart A, chart A st rpt to line E (line C, end of st rpt), Instep chart, chart B from line F (line D, beg of st rpt) to end of st rpt, then full chart B.

Total 56 (62, 72) sts remain.

Notes: (1) When bias panels converge at center front or diverge at center back, some SR segments will span needle intersections. Work them to the lengths shown on Instep charts. (2) When SR segment spans center front on Rnd 24 (24 & 40, 24), work instep CDD only once.

ANKLE
Continue as established using charts for your size — full chart A, chart A st rpt to line E (line C, end of st rpt), Center Front Stitch chart, chart B from line F (line D, beg of st rpt) to end of st rpt, then full chart B — until sock measures 5.5" (6", 6.5") [14cm (15cm, 16.5cm)] above sole.

LEG
Decide whether you need calf expansion (see page 179 for options). If not, work as for ankle for about 1.5" (2", 2.5") [4cm (5cm, 6.5cm)] or length desired. Work last rnd in CC but omit short rows.

Calf expansion by st increases: Continue in pattern but increase one stitch at symmetrical places on each side of center back about every 4th round. Mirror them if you like, such as M1F on righthand side of center back and M1B on lefthand side. Make as many or as few increases as desired, but keep them mostly on the back half of the sock. When they occur on the bias panels, remember that you will have more sts between pattern increases and decreases on those panels. It's helpful to mark the increases with a pin after you make them, to keep track of how many extra stitches each panel has.

After the calf increases, continue to maintain stitch pattern through Rnd 78 (80, 84) or length desired, working last round in CC but omitting short rows.

CUFF
Finish socks with cuff of your choice in CC; see page 180 for options. Cuffs shown are: 4-st cord BO and three ridges of garter stitch (one ridge = k one rnd, p next rnd).

FINISHING
Sew in yarn tails on WS, snugging up last st of foot join graft with tail hanging there.

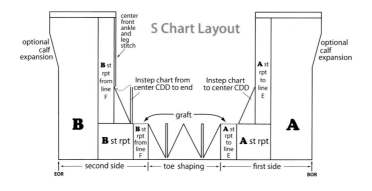

S Chart Layout

optional calf expansion

center front ankle and leg stitch

B st rpt from line F

Instep chart from center CDD to end

Instep chart to center CDD

A st rpt to line E

optional calf expansion

B

B st rpt

B st rpt from line F

graft

A st rpt to line E

A st rpt

A

EOR | second side | toe shaping | first side | BOR

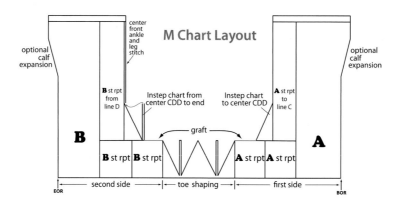

M Chart Layout

optional calf expansion

center front ankle and leg stitch

B st rpt from line D

Instep chart from center CDD to end

Instep chart to center CDD

A st rpt to line C

optional calf expansion

B

B st rpt | **B** st rpt

graft

A st rpt | **A** st rpt

A

EOR | second side | toe shaping | first side | BOR

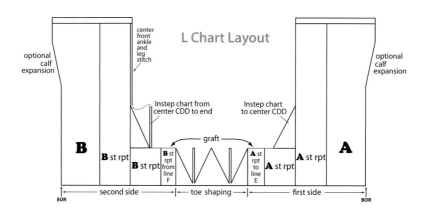

L Chart Layout

optional calf expansion

center front ankle and leg stitch

Instep chart from center CDD to end

Instep chart to center CDD

optional calf expansion

B

B st rpt

B st rpt

B st rpt from line F

graft

A st rpt to line E

A st rpt

A st rpt

A

EOR | second side | toe shaping | first side | BOR

Note: Use decrease symbols in black and color for your size only.
Treat as blank any squares which contain symbols for other sizes.

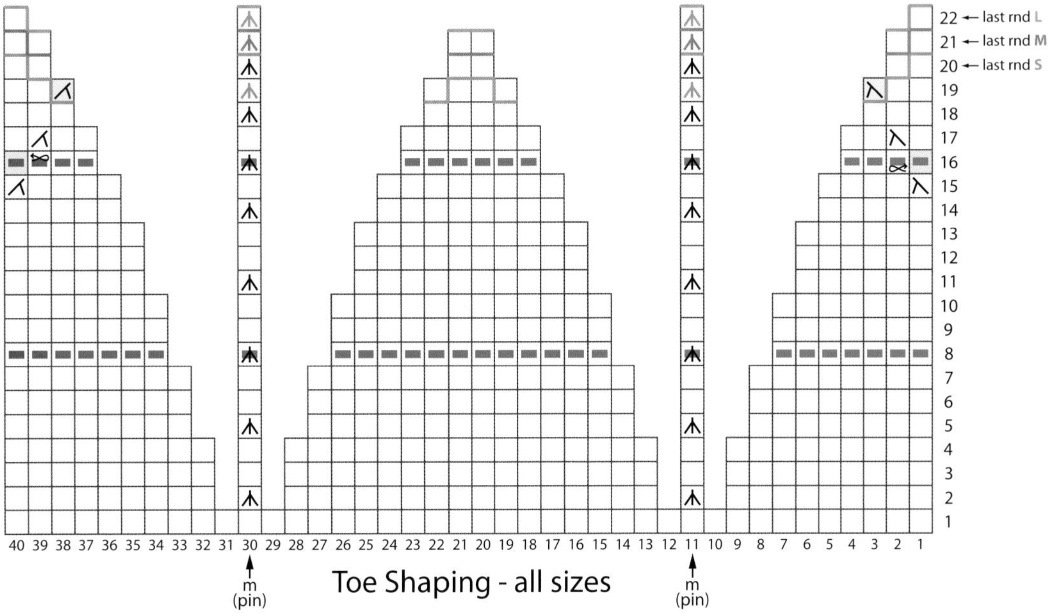

22 ← last rnd L
21 ← last rnd M
20 ← last rnd S
19
18
17
16
15
14
13
12
11
10
9
8
7
6
5
4
3
2
1

40 39 38 37 36 35 34 33 32 31 30 29 28 27 26 25 24 23 22 21 20 19 18 17 16 15 14 13 12 11 10 9 8 7 6 5 4 3 2 1

m
(pin)

Toe Shaping - all sizes

m
(pin)

☐ k MC

▦ k CC on RS, p CC on WS

⧈ w&t, p

⧉ w&t, k

— end L

— end M

— end S

◹ k2tog

◸ ssk

⋏ (any color) CDD

▨ short row

☐ for M & L only;
ignore for S

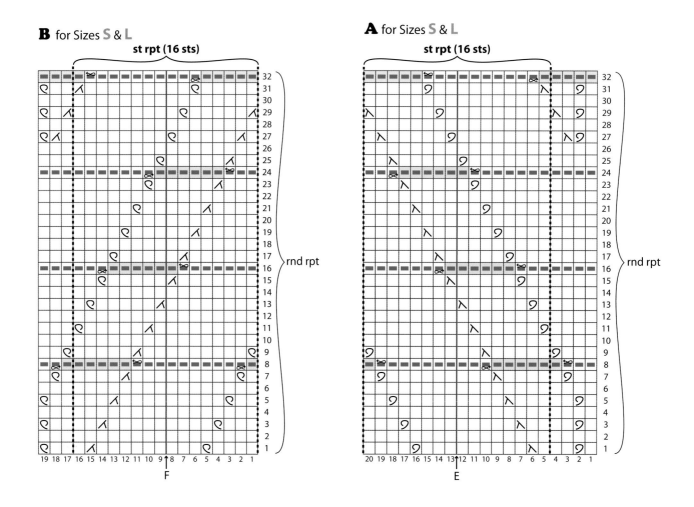

B for Sizes **S** & **L**

A for Sizes **S** & **L**

> "
>
> It is not because things are
> difficult that we do not dare; it
> is because we do not dare that
> they are difficult.
>
> Seneca
>
> "

B for Size **M**

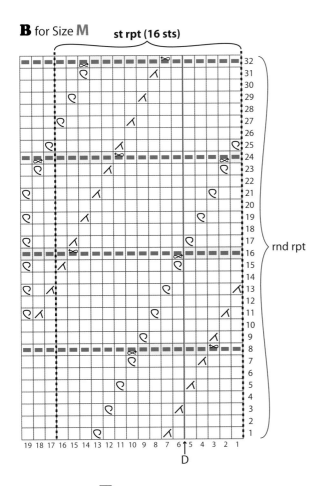

A for Size **M**

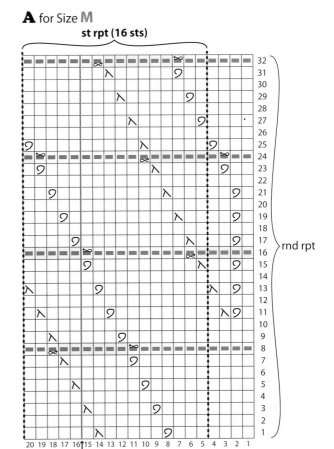

☐ k MC

▬ k CC on RS, p CC on WS

Ϙ M1L

ϱ M1R

⟋ k2tog

⟍ ssk

▢ short row

⧓ w&t, p

⧓ w&t, k

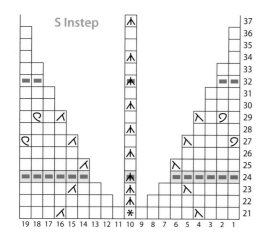

S Instep

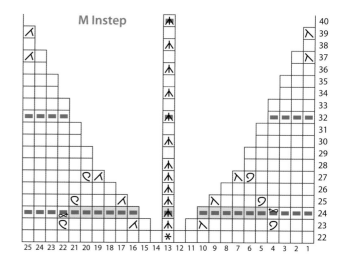

M Instep

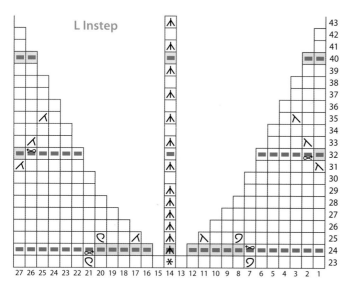

L Instep

Legend

k MC	
k CC on RS, p CC on WS	
M1L	
M1R	
k2tog	
ssk	
short row	
w&t, p	
w&t, k	
(any color) CDD	
✱	see Grafted Foot Join in instructions

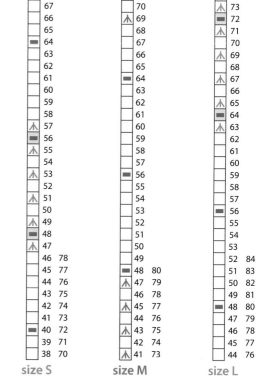

size S		size M		size L	
69		72		75	
68		71		74	
67		70		73	
66		69		72	
65		68		71	
64		67		70	
63		66		69	
62		65		68	
61		64		67	
60		63		66	
59		62		65	
58		61		64	
57		60		63	
56		59		62	
55		58		61	
54		57		60	
53		56		59	
52		55		58	
51		54		57	
50		53		56	
49		52		55	
48		51		54	
47		50		53	
46	78	49		52	84
45	77	48	80	51	83
44	76	47	79	50	82
43	75	46	78	49	81
42	74	45	77	48	80
41	73	44	76	47	79
40	72	43	75	46	78
39	71	42	74	45	77
38	70	41	73	44	76

Center Front Stitch (ankle & leg)

Flaming Arrows

Simple chevrons made by alternating paired increases with paired decreases get an interesting design enhancement through the use of a long-repeat variegated yarn. The layers of color form peaks and valleys on the leg and concentric semicircles on the toe. The lines of paired decreases closest to the toes are masters of illusion; they look like they're just maintaining the chevron pattern, but they're surreptitiously helping to shape the toe at the same time. The zigzag edge at the cuff is an added bonus of a chevron pattern stitch.

Measurements
(lightly blocked)

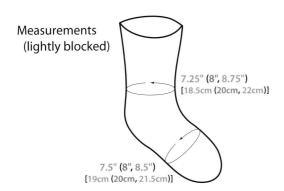

7.25" (8", 8.75")
[18.5cm (20cm, 22cm)]

7.5" (8", 8.5")
[19cm (20cm, 21.5cm)]

Notes

- The finished socks will need to be blocked to nudge the peaks and valleys into place at the sole perimeter and foot join.
- This design is suitable for any variegated yarn: it will accommodate high or low color contrast, as well as long, short, or no color repeats. Different colors inspire different names; see the swatches on page 94.

Yarn

Shown here:
- *Zitron Trekking Maxima;* 75% Superwash New Wool / 25% Nylon; 3.5 oz [100g], 459 yds [420 meters]; 1 (1, 2) balls color 904 (MC)
- *Rowan Kidsilk Haze (optional reinforcement for sole);* 70% super kid mohair / 30% silk; 0.88 oz [25g], 230 yds [210 meters]; color 596; about 0.28 oz [8g] needed for women's medium

Needles

Change needle size if necessary to get the gauge given.
- US size 1½ [2.5mm] — your choice: one long circular at least 40" [100cm], two shorter circulars, or dpns
- one dpn US size 1½ [2.5mm] — not needed if you're already using dpns

Notions

- stitch markers (2 pin-type, 4 any type in 3 colors: c1, c2, c3), tapestry needle

Gauge

- with reinforcing yarn on sole: 32 sts = 4" [10cm], 40 rnds = 4" [10cm]
- without reinforcing yarn, in pattern, unblocked: 40 sts = 4" [10cm], 42 rnds = 4" [10cm]

Size

small (S) - sole about 8.75" [22cm] long, for women's US shoe size 5-6 [Eur size 35/36]

medium (M) - sole about 9.5" [24cm] long, for women's US shoe size 7-8 [Eur size 37/38]

large (L) - sole about 10.25" [26cm] long, for women's US shoe size 9-10 [Eur size 39/40]

SOLE

Holding MC and reinforcement yarn (optional) together and using a variation of JMCO (page 181), cast on 46 (50, 54) pairs of sts on 2 needle points. Total 92 (100, 108) sts.

Rnd 1 (set-up):
Needle 1: K1, M1F, k1, pm c1 for end of heel, k41 (45, 49), pm c2 for beginning of toe, k3. Needle 2: K1, M1L, k1, pm c2 for end of toe, k41 (45, 49), pm c3 for beginning of heel and BOR (3 sts remain on LN after BOR marker). There are 6 heel sts, 6 toe sts, and 41 (45, 49) sts on each side. Total 94 (102, 110) sts.

Rnds 2 - 12 (14, 16):
Work Sole Heel chart between c3 and c1 markers, k41 (45, 49) side sts, work Sole Toe chart between c2 markers including SRs (page 184) as shown, and k41 (45, 49) side sts. Then k17 (20, 22) to center heel (new BOR for rest of sock). Total 154 (172, 190) sts.

Rnd 13 (15, 17):
Note: This round does not appear on Sole Toe and Sole Heel charts. Removing markers as you go, adjust st count for sock top as follows: k22 (23, 25), M1F, [k5 (7, 10), M1F] 22 (18, 14) times, end k22 (23, 25). Cut reinforcing yarn. Total 177 (191, 205) sts.

FOOT

Toe Shaping

Refer to Chart Layout diagram. From center heel BOR with MC, work as follows:

Rnd 1 (set-up):
First side: Work chart A for your size 3 times, then to line B. Total 64 (71, 78) sts.
Toe, all sizes: Work Toe Shaping chart (place markers where indicated). Total 50 sts.
Second side: Work from line C on chart A for your size, then full chart 3 times. Total 63 (70, 77) sts.

Rnds 2-23 (24, 25):
First side: Work chart A for your size 3 times, then to line B.
Toe, all sizes: Work Toe Shaping chart.
Second side: Work from line C on chart A for your size, then full chart A 3 times.

Total 129 (143, 157) sts remain.

Sole Toe - all sizes

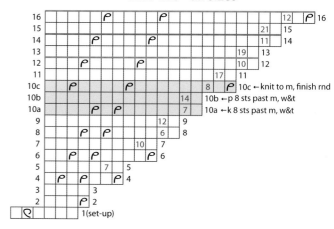

Sole Heel - all sizes

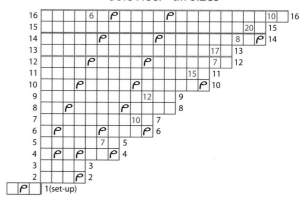

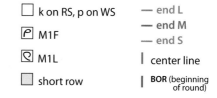

	k on RS, p on WS		— end L
	M1F		— end M
	M1L		— end S
	short row		center line
			BOR (beginning of round)

Chart notes:
Brown numbers give stitch counts greater than 5 to next symbol or end of chart.

After set-up round, work each row of chart twice; first from right to left, then from left to right.

OPTIONAL: When working from left to right, use M1B instead of M1F.

ZIP LINE

Rnd 24 (25, 26):
Work chart A for your size 2 times, then work to * on Instep chart for your size.
Note: The * represents all sts in the zip line join; they do not appear individually on Instep charts.

Join sides of lower foot: Drop working yarn and sl next 14 (17, 20) sts to RN. [If using circular needle(s), don't pull sts on RN to the cable yet.] Slip next 16 (19, 22) sts from LN to dpn (temporary LN). Cut a separate strand of MC about 18" long. Leaving a 4" tail, k2tog. Slip st just made back to LN without turning it. Then make a zip line up the foot with that separate strand by doing the following three steps 13 (16, 19) times:
1. sl 1 st from RN to LN
2. CDD with next 3 sts
3. sl st just made back to LN

Then do step 1 again, drop separate strand, pick up MC working yarn and do last zip CDD with it.

Finish round as follows: Continue to left side of Instep chart, work chart A from line D, then full chart A once. Total 100 (108, 116) sts remain.

Use a pin to mark center front stitch coming from zip line and position it as first st on LN. It will be the center of instep-shaping CDDs. See page 179 for handling a CDD that spans a needle intersection.

INSTEP

Rnds 25-40 (26-42, 27-45):
Using charts for your size, work chart A 2 times, Instep chart, chart A from line D, then full chart A once. Total 72 (80, 88) sts remain.

ANKLE

Work chart A for your size 4 times on each rnd until sock measures 5.5" (6", 6.5") [14cm (15cm, 16.5cm)] above sole.

LEG

Decide whether you need calf expansion (see page 179 for options). If not, work as for ankle for about 1.5" (2", 2.5") [4cm (5cm, 6.5cm)] or desired length.

Calf expansion by st increases: Continue in pattern but increase one stitch at symmetrical places on each side of center back about every 4th round. Mirror them if you like, such as M1F on righthand side of center back and M1B on lefthand side. Make as many or as few increases as desired, but keep them mostly on the back half of the sock. It's helpful to mark the increases with a pin after you make them, to keep track of how many extra stitches each area has.

After the calf increases, continue to maintain stitch pattern to length desired.

CUFF

Finish socks with cuff of your choice; see page 180 for options. Cuffs shown are 4-st cord BO.

FINISHING

Sew in yarn tails on WS, snugging up last st of zip line with tail hanging there.

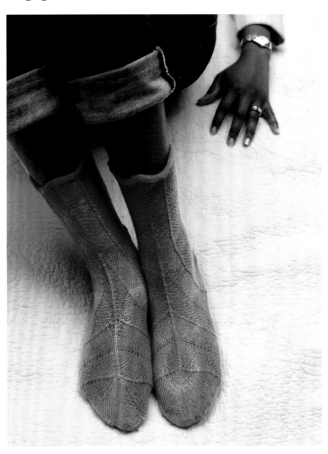

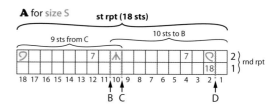

A for size S   st rpt (18 sts)

9 sts from C   10 sts to B

| 9 | | | | | | 7 | ʌ | | | | | | | 7 | Q | 2 } rnd rpt |

18 17 16 15 14 13 12 10 9 8 7 6 5 4 3 2 1   18   1

B C   D

"Black Hills"; Regia 4-Fach Haltbar; 75% Superwash New Wool / 25% Polyamid; 1.75 oz [50g], 230 yds [210 meters]; color 04228.

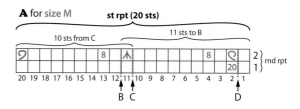

A for size M   st rpt (20 sts)

10 sts from C   11 sts to B

| 9 | | | | | 8 | ʌ | | | | | | | | 8 | Q | 2 } rnd rpt |

20 19 18 17 16 15 14 12 11 10 9 8 7 6 5 4 3 2 1   20   1

B C   D

"Fall Forest"; Abstract Fiber Supersock; 100% Superwash Merino; 3.5 oz [100g], 282 yds [350 meters]; color Hopworks.

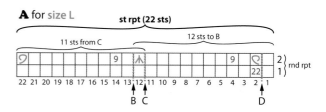

A for size L   st rpt (22 sts)

11 sts from C   12 sts to B

| 9 | | | | | | 9 | ʌ | | | | | | | | | 9 | Q | 2 } rnd rpt |

22 21 20 19 18 17 16 15 14 13 12 11 10 9 8 7 6 5 4 3 2 1   22   1

B C   D

"Surf's Up!"; Zitron Trekking Hand Art; 75% Superwash New Wool / 25% Nylon; 3.5 oz [100g], 459 yds [420 meters]; color Sansibar.

Chart Layout
(all sizes)

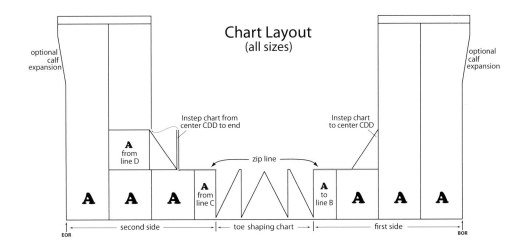

Note: Use decrease symbols in black and color for your size only.
Treat as blank any squares which contain symbols for other sizes.

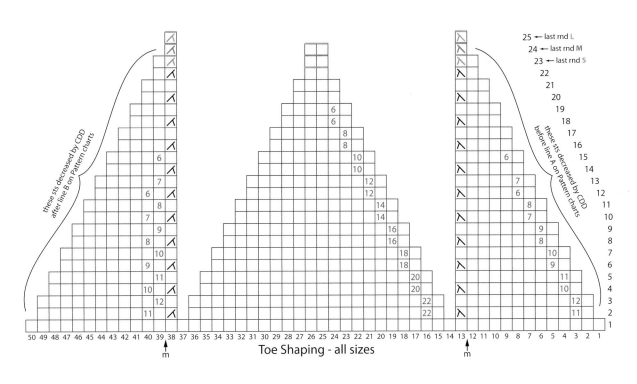

Toe Shaping - all sizes

	knit		(any color) M1R	— end L
	(any color) k2tog		(any color) M1L	— end M
	(any color) ssk		(any color) CDD	— end S

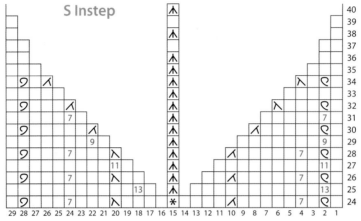

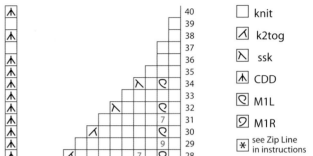

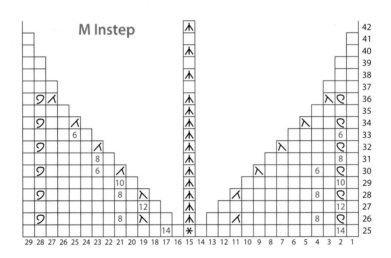

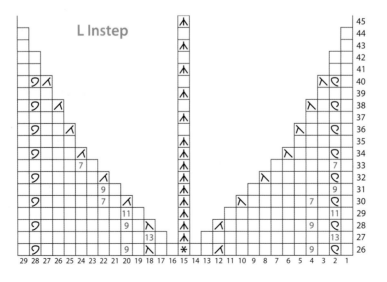

S Instep

M Instep

L Instep

knit

k2tog

ssk

CDD

M1L

M1R

see Zip Line
in instructions

"

We do not see things as they
are; we see them as we are.

Anais Nin

"

COLOR
STRANDING

Fair Isle Trellis

This member of the Trellis Quartet evokes a lush midsummer garden in deep, cooling shade. I designed the toe-shaping decrease lines to complement the stitch pattern and to nudge the diamonds of the trellis into a half-star around the toe. The decreases at the instep bend the diagonal lines of color into graceful, symmetrical arcs. There's a lot to see when you look down on these socks from above.

Measurements
(lightly blocked)

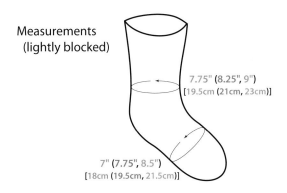

7.75" (8.25", 9")
[19.5cm (21cm, 23cm)]

7" (7.75", 8.5")
[18cm (19.5cm, 21.5cm)]

Note
• On the rounds that have yarn floats of five stitches, it's a good idea to catch in the floats with the working yarn in the middle of those five stitches. Traditionally, floats in Fair Isle knitting can be five stitches long without catching them in, but this is a sock, after all. You don't want to snag your toes in yarn floats when you put on your socks.

Yarn
Shown here:
• *Wonderland Dyeworks fingering weight;* 80% Superwash merino / 20% nylon; 3.5 oz [100g], 400 yds [366 meters]; 1 (1, 1) skein Ocean Cliff (MC)
• *Lorna's Laces Shepard Sock; 80% Superwash wool / 20% polyamide;* 1.75 oz [50g], 215 yds [197 meters]; 1 (1, 1) skein Chino (CC)
• *Rowan Kidsilk Haze (optional reinforcement for sole);* 70% super kid mohair / 30% silk; 0.88 oz [25g], 230 yds [210 meters]; color 629; about 0.28 oz [8g] needed for women's medium

Needles
Change needle size if necessary to get the gauge given.
• US size 1½ [2.5mm] — your choice : one long circular at least 40" [100cm], two shorter circulars, or dpns
• one dpn US size 1½ [2.5mm] — not needed if you're already using dpns

Notions
• stitch markers (2 pin-type, 4 any type in 3 colors: c1, c2, c3), tapestry needle

Gauge
• with reinforcing yarn on sole: 32 sts = 4" [10cm], 40 rnds = 4" [10cm]
• without reinforcing yarn, in pattern, unblocked: 34 sts = 4" [10cm], 36 rnds = 4" [10cm]

Size
small (S) - sole about 8.75" [22cm] long, for women's US shoe size 5-6 [Eur size 35/36]
medium (M) - sole about 9.5" [24cm] long, for women's US shoe size 7-8 [Eur size 37/38]
large (L) - sole about 10.25" [26cm] long, for women's US shoe size 9-10 [Eur size 39/40]

SOLE

Holding MC and reinforcement yarn (optional) together and using a variation of JMCO (page 181), cast on 46 (50, 54) pairs of sts on 2 needle points. Total 92 (100, 108) sts.

Rnd 1 (set-up):
Needle 1: K1, M1F, k1, pm c1 for end of heel, k41 (45, 49), pm c2 for beginning of toe, k3. Needle 2: K1, M1L, k1, pm c2 for end of toe, k41 (45, 49), pm c3 for beginning of heel and BOR (3 sts remain on LN after BOR marker). There are 6 heel sts, 6 toe sts, and 41 (45, 49) sts on each side. Total 94 (102, 110) sts.

Rnds 2 - 12 (14, 16):
Work Sole Heel chart between c3 and c1 markers, k41 (45, 49) side sts, work Sole Toe chart between c2 markers including SRs (page 184) as shown, and k41 (45, 49) side sts. Then k17 (20, 22) to center heel (new BOR for rest of sock). Total 154 (172, 190) sts.

Rnd 13 (15, 17):
Note: This round does not appear on Sole Toe and Sole Heel charts. Removing markers as you go, adjust st count for sock top as follows: k50 (55, 60), M1F, k54 (62, 70), M1F, end k50 (55, 60). Cut reinforcing yarn. Total 156 (174, 192) sts.

FOOT

Toe Shaping
Refer to Chart Layout diagram for your size. From center heel BOR with MC and CC, work as follows:

Rnd 1 (set-up):
First side: Work chart A from BOR for your size to end of st rpt, then st rpt 7 (9, 10) times. Total 51 (60, 69) sts.
Toe, all sizes: Work Toe Shaping chart (place markers where indicated). Total 60 sts.
Second side: Work st rpt of chart A 7 (9, 10) times. For S & L, work left extension of chart A. Total 45 (54, 63) sts.

Rnds 2 - 17 (18, 19):
First side: Work chart A from BOR for your size to end of st rpt, then st rpt 7 (9, 10) times.
Toe, all sizes: Work Toe Shaping chart.
Second side: Work st rpt of chart A 7 (9, 10) times. For S & L, work left extension of chart A.

Total 104 (122, 140) sts remain.

Sole Toe - all sizes

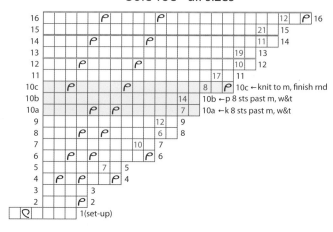

Sole Heel - all sizes

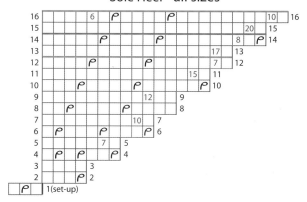

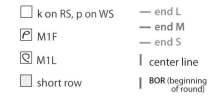

□ k on RS, p on WS — end L
℘ M1F — end M
℧ M1L — end S
□ short row | center line
|| BOR (beginning of round)

Chart notes:

Brown numbers give stitch counts greater than 5 to next symbol or end of chart.

After set-up round, work each row of chart twice; first from right to left, then from left to right.

OPTIONAL: When working from left to right, use M1B instead of M1F.

ZIP LINE

Rnd 18 (19, 20):

Work chart A from BOR for your size to end of st rpt, then st rpt 4 (5, 5) times. Work to * on Instep chart for your size.
Note: The * represents all sts in the zip line join; they do not appear individually on instep charts.

Join sides of lower foot: Drop working yarn and sl next 11 (14, 17) sts to RN. [If using circular needle(s), don't pull sts on RN to the cable yet.] Slip next 12 (15, 18) to dpn (temporary LN). Cut a separate strand of CC about 18" long. Leaving a 4" tail and starting at toe end, make a zip line up the foot by doing the following three steps 10 (13, 16) times:

1. sl 1 st from RN to LN
2. CDD with next 3 sts
3. sl st just made back to LN

Then do step 1 again, drop the separate strand, pick up CC working yarn and do last CDD with it.

Finish round as follows: With MC and CC working yarns, continue to left side of Instep chart, work st rpt of chart A 4 (5, 5) times. For S & L, work left extension of chart A. Total 82 (94, 106) sts remain.

Use a pin to mark center front stitch coming from zip line and position it as first st on LN. It will be the center of instep-shaping CDDs. See page 179 for handling a CDD that spans a needle intersection.

INSTEP

Rnds 19-32 (20-36, 21-40):

Work chart A from BOR for your size to end of st rpt, then st rpt 4 (5, 5) times, Instep chart for your size, st rpt of chart A 4 (5, 5) times. For S & L, work left extension of chart A. Total 66 (72, 78) sts remain.

ANKLE

Remove marker from instep-shaping CDD stitch. Continue as established — chart A from BOR for your size to end of st rpt, st rpt 9 (11, 11) times, then, for S & L only, left extension of chart A — until sock measures 5.5" (6", 6.5") [14cm (15cm, 16.5cm)] above sole.

LEG

Decide whether you need calf expansion (see page 179 for options). If not, work as for ankle for about 1.5" (2", 2.5")

[4cm (5cm, 6.5cm)] or desired length. End having worked Rnd 6 or 12 of chart A.

Calf expansion by st increases: Work to end of Rnd 6 (12, 6) of chart A.

Rnds 1-22:

Work Calf Shaping chart from BOR to line for your size, st rpt of chart A 10 (10, 12) times, then Calf Shaping chart from line for your size to BOR. Total 78 (84, 90) sts.

End leg here or continue in pattern to length desired. End having worked Rnd 6 or 12 of chart A.

CUFF

Finish socks with cuff of your choice; see page 180 for options. Cuffs shown are 4-st cord BO.

FINISHING

Sew in yarn tails on WS, snugging up last st of the zip line with tail hanging there.

> "
> The difference between perseverance and obstinacy is that one comes from a strong will and the other from a strong won't.
>
> Henry Ward Beecher
> "

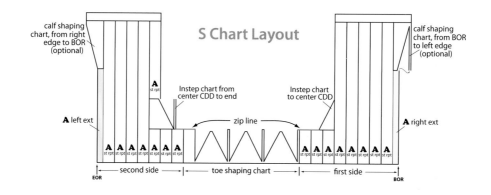

S Chart Layout

calf shaping chart, from right edge to BOR (optional)

calf shaping chart, from BOR to left edge (optional)

A st rpt

Instep chart from center CDD to end

Instep chart to center CDD

A left ext

zip line

A right ext

A st rpt · **A** st rpt · st rpt · st rpt · st rpt · st rpt

st rpt · st rpt · **A** st rpt · **A** st rpt · **A** st rpt · **A** st rpt

EOR — second side — toe shaping chart — first side — BOR

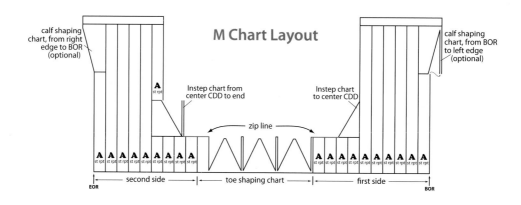

M Chart Layout

calf shaping chart, from right edge to BOR (optional)

calf shaping chart, from BOR to left edge (optional)

A st rpt

Instep chart from center CDD to end

Instep chart to center CDD

zip line

A st rpt · **A** st rpt · **A** st rpt · **A** st rpt · st rpt · st rpt · st rpt · **A** st rpt

st rpt · **A** st rpt · **A** st rpt · **A** st rpt · **A** st rpt · **A** st rpt · **A** st rpt · **A** st rpt

EOR — second side — toe shaping chart — first side — BOR

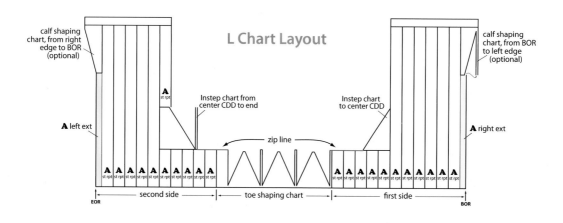

L Chart Layout

calf shaping chart, from right edge to BOR (optional)

calf shaping chart, from BOR to left edge (optional)

A st rpt

Instep chart from center CDD to end

Instep chart to center CDD

A left ext

zip line

A right ext

A st rpt · **A** st rpt · **A** st rpt · **A** st rpt · **A** st rpt · st rpt · st rpt

st rpt · **A** st rpt · **A** st rpt · **A** st rpt · **A** st rpt · **A** st rpt · **A** st rpt · **A** st rpt

EOR — second side — toe shaping chart — first side — BOR

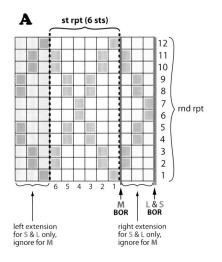

A

st rpt (6 sts)

rnd rpt

left extension
for **S & L** only,
ignore for **M**

M
BOR

L & S
BOR

right extension
for **S & L** only,
ignore for **M**

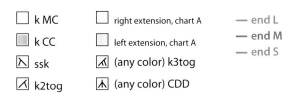

☐ k MC   ☐ right extension, chart A   — end L

▨ k CC   ☐ left extension, chart A   — end M

◩ ssk   ◪ (any color) k3tog   — end S

◪ k2tog   ⋏ (any color) CDD

Note: Use decrease symbols in black and color for your size only.
Treat as blank any squares which contain symbols for other sizes.

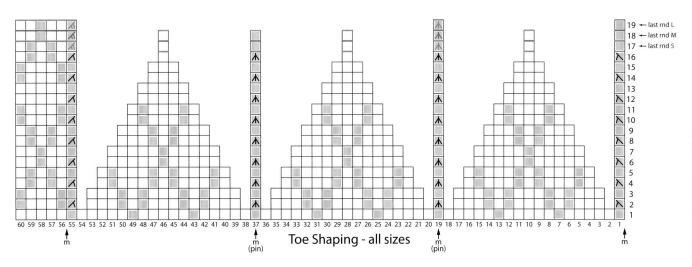

Toe Shaping - all sizes

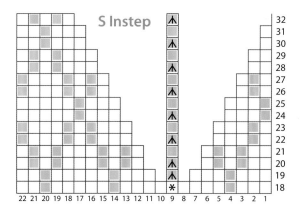

S Instep

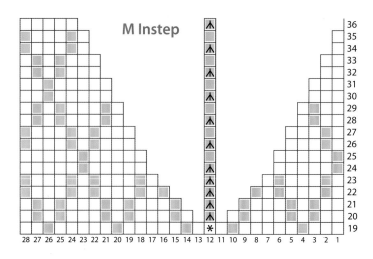

M Instep

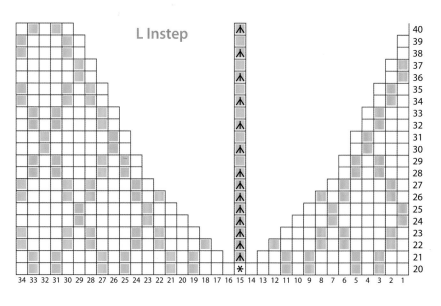

L Instep

Calf Shaping - all sizes

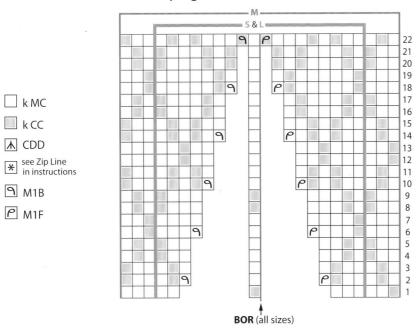

M

S & L

k MC
k CC
CDD
see Zip Line in instructions
M1B
M1F

22
21
20
19
18
17
16
15
14
13
12
11
10
9
8
7
6
5
4
3
2
1

BOR (all sizes)

Louvered Light

These Crazyfoot colors just sing to me of peaceful warmth and cozy comfort. And the stitch pattern expresses a harmonizing vision of sunset through slanted window blinds or glowing embers through sleepy eyelashes. The pattern repeat is equally relaxing: three stitches of each color on every round. Slanting the color lines gives movement to the design, and mirror imaging the sides balances that movement and gives it closure at the center front and back.

Note

- Grafting in pattern at the foot join might be worth the effort on this design, because (1) it keeps the louver lines unbroken and (2) the simplicity of the color pattern makes grafting in pattern easier than it usually is. Thread a length of each color on a separate yarn needle and graft with whichever color would come next in the pattern if you were knitting rather than grafting.
- On one sock I allowed the zip line and centered double decreases of the instep-shaping to form a dark line at center foot and ankle. On the other sock I eliminated the dark line by grafting the foot join and shaping the instep with paired single decreases (see page 17, CDD Ridge). Maybe you can decide which you like better; I can't.

Yarn

Shown here:
- *Mountain Colors Crazyfoot;* 90% Superwash Merino Wool / 10% nylon; 3.5 oz [100g], 425 yds [388 meters]; 1 (1, 1) skein Yellowstone (MC)
- *Malabrigo Sock; 100% Superwash Merino Wool;* 3.5 oz [100g], 440 yds [402 meters]; 1 (1, 1) skein 812 Chocolate Amargo (CC)
- *Rowan Kidsilk Haze (optional reinforcement for sole);* 70% super kid mohair / 30% silk; 0.88 oz [25g], 230 yds [210 meters]; color 584; about 0.28 oz [8g] needed for women's medium

Needles

Change needle size if necessary to get gauge given.
- US size 1½ [2.5mm] for sole with reinforcing yarn — your choice: one long circular at least 40" [100cm], two shorter circulars, or dpns
- US size 1 [2.25mm] for sock top — your choice: one long circular at least 40" [100cm], two shorter circulars, or dpns
- one dpn US size 1 [2.25mm] — not needed if you're already using dpns

Notions

- stitch markers (2 pin-type, 4 any type in 3 colors: c1, c2, c3), tapestry needle

Gauge

- with reinforcing yarn on sole: 32 sts = 4" [10cm], 40 rnds = 4" [10cm]
- without reinforcing yarn, in pattern, unblocked: 37 sts = 4" [10cm], 45 rnds = 4" [10cm]

Size

small (S) - sole about 8.75" [22cm] long, for women's US shoe size 5-6 [Eur size 35/36]

medium (M) - sole about 9.5" [24cm] long, for women's US shoe size 7-8 [Eur size 37/38]

large (L) - sole about 10.25" [26cm] long, for women's US shoe size 9-10 [Eur size 39/40]

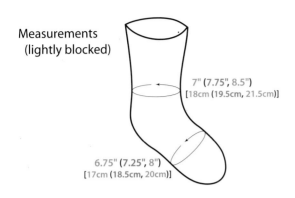

Measurements
(lightly blocked)

7" (7.75", 8.5")
[18cm (19.5cm, 21.5cm)]

6.75" (7.25", 8")
[17cm (18.5cm, 20cm)]

Sole Toe - all sizes

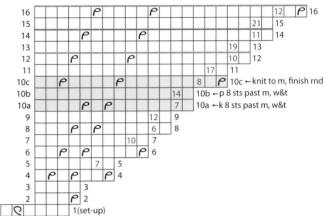

10c ← knit to m, finish rnd
10b ← p 8 sts past m, w&t
10a ← k 8 sts past m, w&t

SOLE

Holding CC and reinforcement yarn (optional) together and using a variation of JMCO (page 181), cast on 46 (50, 54) pairs of sts on 2 needle points. Total 92 (100, 108) sts.

Rnd 1 (set-up):

Needle 1: K1, M1F, k1, pm c1 for end of heel, k41 (45, 49), pm c2 for beginning of toe, k3. Needle 2: K1, M1L, k1, pm c2 for end of toe, k41 (45, 49), pm c3 for beginning of heel and BOR (3 sts remain on LN after BOR marker). There are 6 heel sts, 6 toe sts, and 41 (45, 49) sts on each side. Total 94 (102, 110) sts.

Rnds 2 - 12 (14, 16):

Work Sole Heel chart between c3 and c1 markers, k41 (45, 49) side sts, work Sole Toe chart between c2 markers including SRs (page 184) as shown, and k41 (45, 49) side sts. Then k17 (20, 22) to center heel (new BOR for rest of sock). Total 154 (172, 190) sts.

Rnd 13 (15, 17):

Note: This round does not appear on Sole Toe and Sole Heel charts. Removing markers as you go, adjust st count for sock top as follows: k25 (26, 28), M1F, [k21 (24, 27), M1F] 5 times, end k24 (26, 27). Cut reinforcing yarn. Total 160 (178, 196) sts.

FOOT

Toe Shaping

Refer to Chart Layout diagram for your size. From center heel BOR with 2.25mm needle, work as follows:

Rnd 1 (set-up):

First side: Work chart A from BOR for your size, then st rpt of chart A 8 (10, 11) times. Total 57 (66, 75) sts.

Sole Heel - all sizes

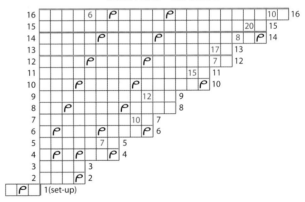

Chart notes:

Brown numbers give stitch counts greater than 5 to next symbol or end of chart.

After set-up round, work each row of chart twice; first from right to left, then from left to right.

OPTIONAL: When working from left to right, use M1B instead of M1F.

Legend

- ☐ k on RS, p on WS
- P M1F
- Q M1L
- ☐ short row

- — end L
- — end M
- — end S
- | center line
- | **BOR** (beginning of round)

Toe, all sizes: Work Toe Shaping chart (place markers where indicated). Total 46 sts.
Second side: Work st rpt of chart B 8 (10, 11) times, then chart B to EOR for your size. Total 57 (66, 75) sts.

Rnds 2 - 19 (20, 21):
First side: Work chart A from BOR for your size, then st rpt of chart A 8 (10, 11) times.
Toe, all sizes: Work Toe Shaping chart.
Second side: Work st rpt of chart B 8 (10, 11) times, then chart B to EOR for your size.

Total 122 (138, 156) sts remain.

ZIP LINE

Rnd 20 (21, 22):
Work chart A from BOR for your size, st rpt of chart A 3 (4, 4) times, then to * on Instep chart for your size.
Note: The * represents all sts in the zip line join; they do not appear individually on instep charts.

Join sides of lower foot: Drop working yarn and sl next 13 (15, 18) sts to RN. [If using circular needle(s), don't pull sts on RN to the cable yet.] Sl next 15 (17, 20) sts to dpn (temporary LN). Cut a separate strand of CC about 18" long. Leaving a 4" tail, k2tog with the separate strand. Slip that st back to LN without turning it. Then make a zip line up the foot with that separate strand by doing the following three steps 12 (14, 17) times:
1. sl 1 st from RN to LN
2. CDD with next 3 sts
3. sl st just made back to LN

Then do step 1 again, drop the separate strand, pick up CC working yarn and do last zip CDD with it.

Finish round as follows: With MC and CC working yarns continue to left side of Instep chart for your size, work st rpt of chart B 4 (5, 5) times, then chart B to EOR for your size. Total 95 (107, 119) sts remain.

Use a pin to mark center front stitch coming from zip line and position it as first st on LN. It will be the center of instep-shaping CDDs. See page 179 for handling a CDD that spans a needle intersection.

INSTEP

Rnds 20-40 (21-43, 22-46):
Work chart A from BOR for your size, st rpt of chart A 3 (4, 4) times, Instep chart for your size, st rpt of chart B 4 (5, 5) times, then chart B to EOR for your size. Total 66 (72, 78) sts remain.

ANKLE

Continue as established — chart A from BOR for your size, st rpt of chart A 4 (5, 5) times, st rpt of chart B 4 (5, 5) times, then chart B to EOR for your size — until sock measures 5.5" (6", 6.5") [14cm (15cm, 16.5cm)] above sole.

LEG

Decide whether you need calf expansion (see page 179 for options). If not, work as for ankle for about 1.5" (2", 2.5") [4cm (5cm, 6.5cm)] or desired length.

Calf expansion by st increases: Work to end of Rnd 2 (Rnd 5, Rnd 2) of charts A and B.

Rnds 1-24:
Work Calf Shaping chart from BOR, chart A 3 (4, 4) times, chart B 3 (4, 4) times, then Calf Shaping chart to BOR. Total 78 (84, 90) sts.

End leg here or continue in pattern as established to length desired.

CUFF

Finish socks with cuff of your choice in CC; see page 180 for options. Cuffs shown are 4-st cord BO and three ridges of garter stitch (one ridge = k one rnd, p next rnd).

FINISHING

Sew in yarn tails on WS, snugging up last st of zip line with tail hanging there.

> "
> ### Art is at its best when it forgets its name.
> Dubuffet
>
> (via American Visionary Art Museum)
>
> "

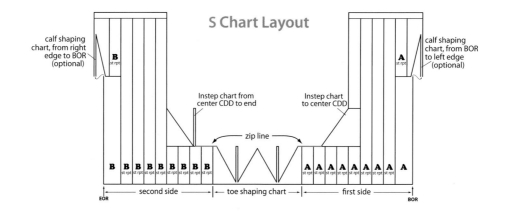

S Chart Layout

calf shaping chart, from right edge to BOR (optional)

B st rpt

Instep chart from center CDD to end

Instep chart to center CDD

calf shaping chart, from BOR to left edge (optional)

A st rpt

zip line

B **B** st rpt **B** st rpt **B** st rpt **B** st rpt **B** st rpt **B** st rpt **B** st rpt **B** st rpt

A st rpt **A** st rpt **A** st rpt **A** st rpt **A** st rpt **A** st rpt **A** st rpt **A** st rpt **A**

EOR ←——— second side ———→ ←— toe shaping chart —→ ←——— first side ———→ BOR

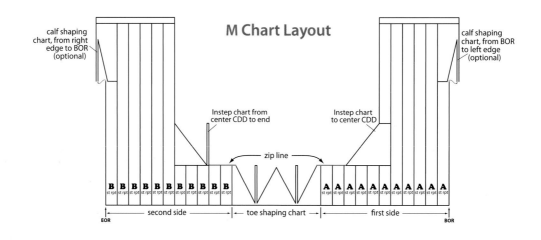

M Chart Layout

calf shaping chart, from right edge to BOR (optional)

Instep chart from center CDD to end

Instep chart to center CDD

calf shaping chart, from BOR to left edge (optional)

zip line

B st rpt **B** st rpt **B** st rpt **B** st rpt **B** st rpt **B** st rpt **B** st rpt **B** st rpt **B** st rpt **B** st rpt **B** st rpt

A st rpt **A** st rpt **A** st rpt **A** st rpt **A** st rpt **A** st rpt **A** st rpt **A** st rpt **A** st rpt **A** st rpt **A**

EOR ←——— second side ———→ ←— toe shaping chart —→ ←——— first side ———→ BOR

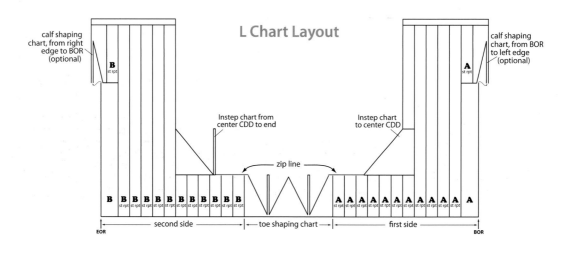

L Chart Layout

calf shaping chart, from right edge to BOR (optional)

B st rpt

Instep chart from center CDD to end

Instep chart to center CDD

calf shaping chart, from BOR to left edge (optional)

A st rpt

zip line

B **B** st rpt **B** st rpt **B** st rpt **B** st rpt **B** st rpt **B** st rpt **B** st rpt **B** st rpt **B** st rpt **B** st rpt **B**

A st rpt **A** st rpt **A** st rpt **A** st rpt **A** st rpt **A** st rpt **A** st rpt **A** st rpt **A** st rpt **A** st rpt **A**

EOR ←——— second side ———→ ←— toe shaping chart —→ ←——— first side ———→ BOR

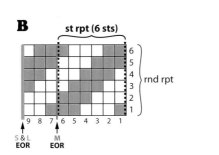

B — st rpt (6 sts)

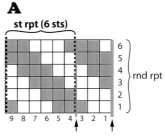

A — st rpt (6 sts)

☐ k MC
▨ k CC
🝆 (any color) ssk
🝆 (any color) k2tog

— end L
— end M
— end S

Note: Use decrease symbols in black and color for your size only.
Treat as blank any squares which contain symbols for other sizes.

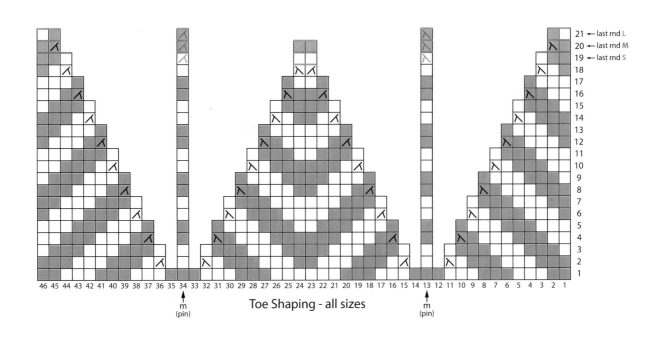

Toe Shaping - all sizes

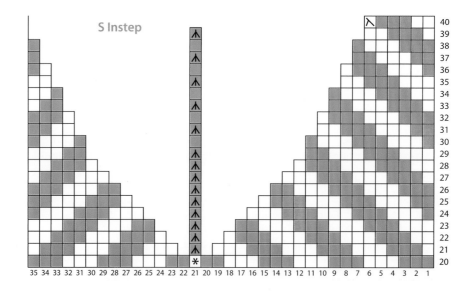

S Instep

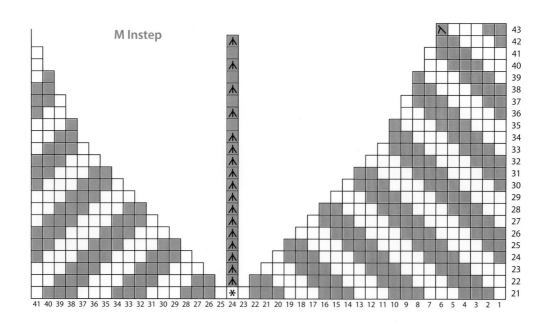

M Instep

	k MC		CDD		M1B
	k CC	✳	see Zip Line in instructions		M1F
	ssk				

L Instep

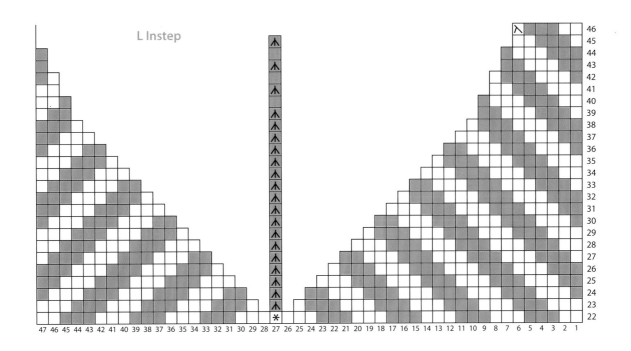

Calf Shaping - all sizes

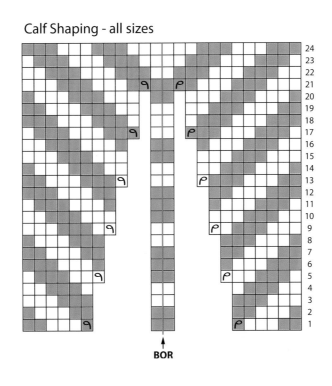

BOR

Fair-gyle

The argyle motif has become a timeless classic. Happily, when rendered as it is here in two-color stranded knitting, popularly known as Fair Isle, no bobbins are required. The red-and-white color scheme has its own timeless appeal, but any colors with good contrast could be used. Hmm, maybe it would be fun to combine one mildly variegated yarn with a coordinating solid....

Measurements
(lightly blocked)

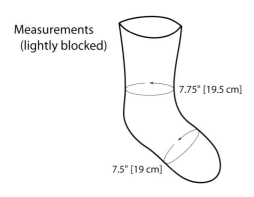

7.75" [19.5 cm]

7.5" [19 cm]

"

A person who has never
made a mistake has never
tried anything new.

Albert Einstein

"

Note
● Only one size is given because of the 22-stitch pattern repeat. Adding one repeat would make the large size very large, and subtracting one repeat would make the small size very small. You can get some size variation by working the pattern as given at a slightly larger or smaller gauge. However, if you do change to thinner or thicker needles, *be sure your yarn is correspondingly thinner or thicker.* Swatching is essential in a case like this, dear knitters, so that you don't end up with either stiff or wimpy socks.

Yarn
Shown here:
● *Shi Bui Sock;* 100% Superwash Merino; 1.75 oz [50g], 191 yds [175 meters]; 2 skeins color 7501 (MC)
● *Miss Babs "Yummy" Monochrome Sock & Baby yarn;* 2-ply Superwash 100% Merino Wool; 4 oz [113 g], 400 yds [365 meters]; 1 skein Sandi's Red (CC)
● *Rowan Kidsilk Haze (optional reinforcement for sole);* 70% super kid mohair / 30% silk; 0.88 oz [25g], 230 yds [210 meters]; color 634; about 0.28 oz [8g] needed for women's medium

Needles
Change needle size if necessary to get gauge given.
● US size 1½ [2.5mm] — your choice: one long circular at least 40" [100cm], two shorter circulars, or dpns
● one dpn US size 1½ [2.5mm] — not needed if you're already using dpns

Notions
● stitch markers (2 pin-type, 4 any type in 3 colors: c1, c2, c3), tapestry needle

Gauge
● with reinforcing yarn on sole: 32 sts = 4" [10cm], 40 rnds = 4" [10cm]
● without reinforcing yarn, in pattern, unblocked: 34 sts = 4" [10cm], 40 rnds = 4" [10cm]

Size
medium - sole about 9.5" [24cm] long, for women's US shoe size 7-8 [Eur size 37/38]

SOLE

Holding MC and reinforcement yarn (optional) together and using a variation of JMCO (page 181), cast on 50 pairs of sts on 2 needle points. Total 100 sts.

Rnd 1 (set-up)

Needle 1: K1, M1F, k1, pm c1 for end of heel, k45, pm c2 for beginning of toe, k3. Needle 2: K1, M1L, k1, pm c2 for end of toe, k45, pm c3 for beginning of heel and BOR (3 sts remain on LN after BOR marker). There are 6 heel sts, 6 toe sts, and 45 sts on each side. Total 102 sts.

Rnds 2-14:

Work Sole Heel chart between c3 and c1 markers, k45 side sts, work Sole Toe chart between c2 markers including SRs (page 184) as shown, and k45 side sts. Then k20 to center heel (new BOR for rest of sock). Total 172 sts.

Rnd 15:

Note: This round does not appear on Sole Toe and Sole Heel charts.

Removing markers as you go, adjust st count for sock top as follows: k23, M1F, (k18, M1F) 7 times, end k23. Cut reinforcing yarn. Total 180 sts.

FOOT

Toe Shaping

Refer to Chart Layout diagram. From center heel BOR with MC and CC, work as follows:

Set-up rnd:

First side: Work st rpt of chart A 3 times. Total 66 sts.
Toe: Work Toe Shaping chart (place markers where indicated). Total 49 sts.
Second side: Work from line B on chart A to end of st rpt, then st rpt 2 times. Total 65 sts.

Rnds 1-17:

First side: Work st rpt of chart A 3 times.
Toe: Work Toe Shaping chart.
Second side: Work from line B on chart A to end of st rpt, then st rpt 2 times.

Total 136 sts remain.

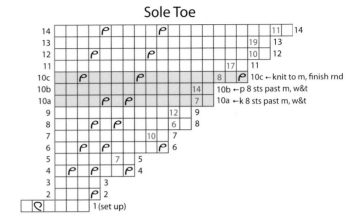

Sole Toe

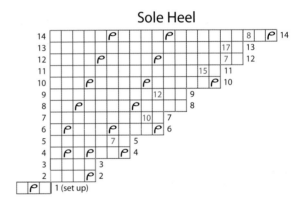

Sole Heel

☐	k MC on RS, p MC on WS	▨	short row
ℙ	M1F	│	center line
ℚ	M1L	▌	**BOR** (beginning of round)

Chart notes:
Brown numbers give stitch counts greater than 5 to next symbol or end of chart.

After set-up round, work each row of chart twice; first from right to left, then from left to right.

OPTIONAL: When working from left to right, use M1B instead of M1F.

ZIP LINE

Rnd 18:

Work full chart A (33 sts), then work to * on Instep chart.
Note: The * represents all sts in the zip line join; they do not appear individually on Instep chart.

Join sides of lower foot: Join the two sides of lower foot as follows: Drop working yarn and sl next 14 sts to RN. [If using circular needle(s), don't pull sts on RN to the cable yet.] Sl next 17 sts to dpn (temporary LN). Cut separate strand of CC about 18" long. Leaving a 4" tail, work first 3 sts on LN as follows: slip1 knitwise, slip 2tog knitwise, k3tog by inserting LN tfl of 3 sts on RN. Slip st just made back to LN without turning it. Then make a zip line up foot with the separate strand by doing the following three steps 13 times:

1. sl 1 st from RN to LN
2. CDD with next 3 sts
3. sl st just made back to LN

Then do step 1 again, drop separate strand, pick up CC working yarn and do last zip CDD with it.

Finish round as follows: With MC and CC working yarns, continue to left side of Instep chart, then work chart A backwards from right side to line B (32 sts). Total 106 sts remain.

Use a pin to mark center front stitch coming from zip line and position it as first st on LN. It will be the center of instep-shaping CDDs. See page 179 for handling a CDD that spans a needle intersection.

INSTEP

Rnds 19-38:

Work full chart A (33 sts), Instep Shaping chart, then chart A backwards from right side to line B (32 sts). Total 66 sts remain.

ANKLE

Work st rpt of chart A 3 times on each rnd until sock measures 6" [15cm] above sole.

LEG

Decide whether you need calf expansion (see page 179 for options). If not, work as for ankle for about 2" [5cm] or desired length. End having worked Rnd 11 or 22 of chart A.

Calf expansion by st increases: Work to end of Rnd 55.

Rnds 56-78:

Work from BOR of Calf Shaping chart to left side, from line B of chart A to end of st rpt, full st rpt 2 times, then from right side of Calf Shaping chart to BOR. Total 78 sts.

CUFF

Knit one rnd in MC. Finish socks with cuff of your choice; see page 180 for options. One cuff shown is 8 rnds of half-twisted ribbing, the other is 8 rnds of seed stitch.

FINISHING

Sew in yarn tails on WS, snugging up last st of zip line with tail hanging there.

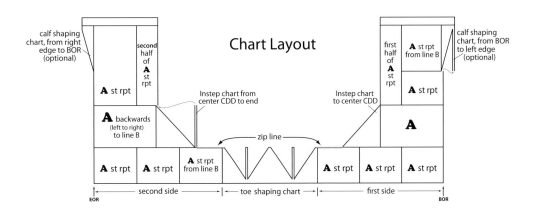

st rpt (22 sts)

for rnds 18 - 38 work chart from right to left on first side, then *left to right on second side*

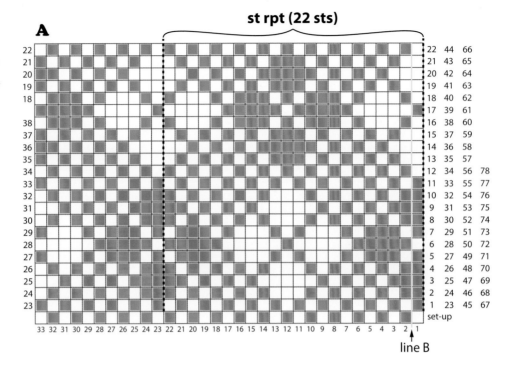

line B

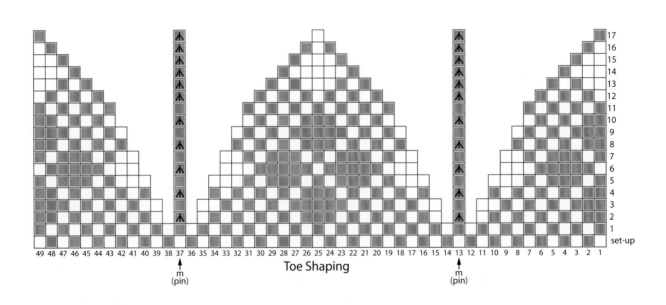

Toe Shaping

m (pin)

Instep

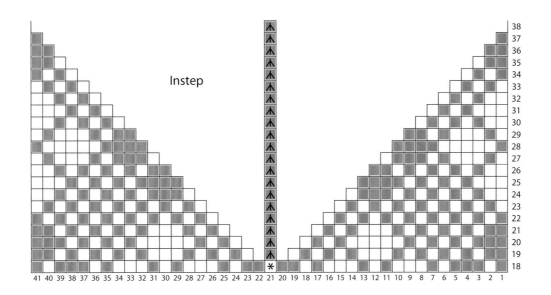

Calf Shaping

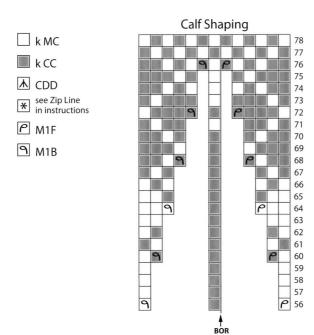

Legend:

- ☐ k MC
- ▨ k CC
- ⋏ CDD
- ✳ see Zip Line in instructions
- ⌐ M1F
- ⌐ M1B

BOR

TRAVELING STITCH

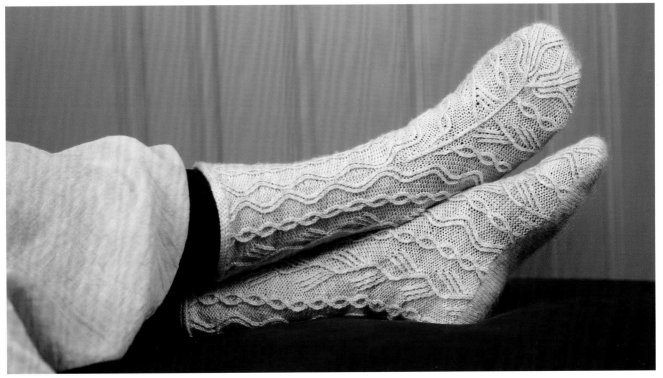

Traveling Trellis

Traveling stitch is a great technique for socks. It makes a sturdy fabric, doesn't curl, has wonderful elasticity, and always looks neat and tailored. It is particularly effective in this third rendering of the trellis theme, because the pattern lines flow smoothly and distinctly against the background. A few flower-colored beads on the leg seem like a natural addition to a trellis, particularly for these socks. After all, anything named "Pond Scum," as this yarn color is, could probably use a little help.

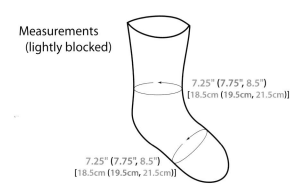

Measurements
(lightly blocked)

7.25" (7.75", 8.5")
[18.5cm (19.5cm, 21.5cm)]

7.25" (7.75", 8.5")
[18.5cm (19.5cm, 21.5cm)]

Notes

- As in the other members of the Trellis Quartet, the toe-decrease lines relate to the trellis lines, but with traveling stitch they blend in perfectly with the stitch pattern because they are twisted like all the other trellis lines.
- You need a cable needle only for the few crosses that span a needle intersection.

Yarn

Shown here:

- *Blue Moon Socks that Rock; 100% superwash merino - lightweight;* 4.5 oz [127g], 360 yds [329 meters]; 1 (1, 2) skeins Pond Scum (MC)
- *Rowan Kidsilk Haze (optional reinforcement for sole);* 70% super kid mohair / 30% silk; 0.88 oz [25g], 230 yds [210 meters]; color 629; about 0.28 oz [8g] needed for women's medium

Needles

Change needle size if necessary to get gauge given.

- US size 1½ [2.5mm] — your choice: one long circular at least 40" [100cm], two shorter circulars, or dpns
- US size 1½ [2.5mm] — not needed if you're already using dpns
- cable needle

Notions

- stitch markers (2 pin-type, 4 any type in 3 colors: c1, c2, c3), tapestry needle, optional beads (example shows 65 size 6 seed beads on one sock; use more or fewer as desired)

Gauge

- with reinforcing yarn on sole: 32 sts = 4" [10cm], 40 rnds = 4" [10cm]
- without reinforcing yarn, in pattern, unblocked: 40 sts = 4" [10cm], 42 rnds = 4" [10cm]

Size

small (S) - sole about 8.75" [22cm] long, for women's US shoe size 5-6 [Eur size 35/36]

medium (M) - sole about 9.5" [24cm] long, for women's US shoe size 7-8 [Eur size 37/38]

large (L) - sole about 10.25" [26cm] long, for women's US shoe size 9-10 [Eur size 39/40]

SOLE

Holding MC and reinforcement yarn (optional) together and using a variation of JMCO (page 181), cast on 46 (50, 54) pairs of sts on 2 needle points. Total 92 (100, 108) sts.

Rnd 1 (set-up):
Needle 1: K1, M1F, k1, pm c1 for end of heel, k41 (45, 49), pm c2 for beginning of toe, k3. Needle 2: K1, M1L, k1, pm c2 for end of toe, k41 (45, 49), pm c3 for beginning of heel and BOR (3 sts remain on LN after BOR marker). There are 6 heel sts, 6 toe sts, and 41 (45, 49) sts on each side. Total 94 (102, 110) sts.

Rnds 2 - 12 (14, 16):
Work Sole Heel chart between c3 and c1 markers, k41 (45, 49) side sts, work Sole Toe chart between c2 markers including SRs (page 184) as shown, and k41 (45, 49) side sts. Then k17 (20, 22) to center heel (new BOR for rest of sock). Total 154 (172, 190) sts.

Rnd 13 (15, 17):
Note: This round does not appear on Sole Toe and Sole Heel charts. Removing markers as you go, adjust st count for sock top as follows: k22 (26, 30), M1F, [k22 (24, 26), M1F] 5 times, end k22 (26, 30). Cut reinforcing yarn. Total 160 (178, 196) sts.

FOOT

Toe Shaping

Refer to Chart Layout diagram for your size. From center heel BOR with MC, work as follows:

Rnd 1 (set-up):
First side: Work chart A from BOR for your size to end of st rpt, then st rpt 8 (9, 11) times. Total 54 (63, 72) sts.
Toe, all sizes: Work Toe Shaping chart (place markers where indicated). Total 52 sts.
Second side: Work st rpt of chart A 9 (10, 12) times. For M, work left extension of chart A. Total 54 (63, 72) sts.

Rnds 2 - 22 (23, 24):
First side: Work chart A from BOR for your size to end of st rpt, then st rpt 8 (9, 11) times.
Toe, all sizes: Work Toe Shaping chart.
Second side: Work st rpt of chart A 9 (10, 12) times. For M, work left extension of chart A.

Total 116 (134, 152) sts remain.

Sole Toe - all sizes

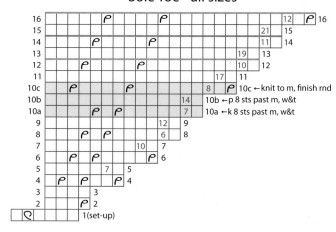

Sole Heel - all sizes

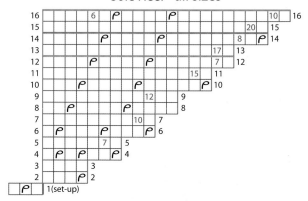

Legend:
- ☐ k on RS, p on WS
- ℙ M1F
- ℚ M1L
- ▨ short row
- — end L
- — end M
- — end S
- | center line
- | BOR (beginning of round)

Chart notes:
Brown numbers give stitch counts greater than 5 to next symbol or end of chart.

After set-up round, work each row of chart twice; first from right to left, then from left to right.

OPTIONAL: When working from left to right, use M1B instead of M1F.

ZIP LINE

Rnd 23 (24, 25):
Work chart A from BOR for your size to end of st rpt, then st rpt 4 (4, 5) times, then work to * on Instep chart for your size. Note: The * represents all sts in the zip line join; they do not appear individually on instep charts.

Join sides of lower foot: Drop working yarn and sl next 12 (16, 19) sts to RN. [If using circular needle(s), don't pull sts on RN to the cable yet.] Sl next 14 (18, 21) sts to dpn (temporary LN). Cut a separate strand of MC about 18" long. Leaving a 4" tail, k2tog tbl with the separate strand. Slip that st back to LN, sl it purlwise tbl, return it to LN in its turned position. Then make a twisted zip line up the foot with that separate strand by doing the following three steps 11 (15, 18) times:
1. sl 1 st from RN to LN
2. CDD with next 3 sts
3. sl st just made back to LN, sl it purlwise tbl, return it to LN in its turned position.

Then do step 1, drop the separate strand, pick up MC working yarn and do last zip CDD tbl with it.

Finish rnd as follows: Continue to left side of Instep chart, st rpt of chart A 5 (5, 6) times. For M, work left extension of chart A. Total 91 (101, 113) sts remain.

Use a pin to mark center front stitch coming from zip line and position it as first st on LN. It will be the center of instep-shaping CDDs. See page 179 for handling a CDD that spans a needle intersection.

INSTEP

Rnds 24-40 (25-42, 26-45):
Work chart A from BOR for your size to end of st rpt, then st rpt 4 (4, 5) times, Instep chart for your size, st rpt of chart A 5 (5, 6) times. For M, work left extension of chart A. Total 72 (78, 84) sts remain.

ANKLE

Continue as established — chart A from BOR for your size to end of st rpt, st rpt 11 (11, 13) times, then left extension of chart A for M only — until sock measures 5.5" (6", 6.5") [14cm (15cm, 16.5cm)] above sole.

Start adding beads in this section, if desired. In the example, the working yarn was cut at the end of Rnd 48, beads strung on it, then the beads were slid into place on the running strand between the 2nd & 3rd purl sts of each purl area on Rnds 50, 56, 62, 68, and 74. Note: Rnds 62, 68, and 74 correspond to Rnds 6, 12, and 18, respectively, on the Calf Shaping charts.

LEG

Decide whether you need calf expansion (see page 179 for options). If not, work as for ankle for about 1.5" (2", 2.5") [4cm (5cm, 6.5cm)] or desired length. End having worked Rnd 3 or 9 of chart A.

Calf expansion by st increases: Work to end of Rnd 2 (Rnd 8, Rnd 2) on chart A.

Rnds 1-25: (Note: During calf shaping, ignore the BOR lines on chart A.) Work Calf Shaping chart for your size from BOR, st rpt of chart A 10 (12, 12) times, then Calf Shaping chart for your size to BOR. Total 78 (84, 90) sts.

CUFF

Finish socks with cuff of your choice; see page 180 for options. One cuff shown is 4-st cord BO and the other is 6 rnds of k2 tbl, p1 ribbing coordinated with stitch pattern (see Ribbing chart, page 131).

FINISHING

Sew in yarn tails on WS, snugging up last st of zip line with tail hanging there.

> " Living is like
> licking honey off a thorn.
> Louis Adamic's grandfather
> "

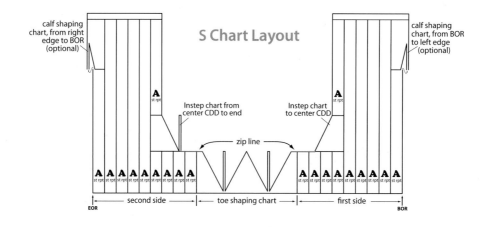

S Chart Layout

calf shaping chart, from right edge to BOR (optional)

calf shaping chart, from BOR to left edge (optional)

A st rpt

A st rpt

Instep chart from center CDD to end

Instep chart to center CDD

zip line

A **A** **A** **A** **A** **A** **A** **A**
st rpt st rpt st rpt st rpt st rpt st rpt st rpt st rpt

A **A** **A** **A** **A** **A** **A** **A**
st rpt st rpt st rpt st rpt st rpt st rpt st rpt st rpt

second side

toe shaping chart

first side

EOR

BOR

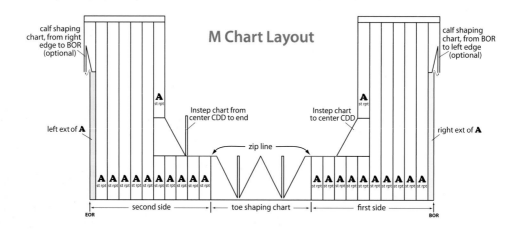

M Chart Layout

calf shaping chart, from right edge to BOR (optional)

calf shaping chart, from BOR to left edge (optional)

A st rpt

A st rpt

left ext of **A**

right ext of **A**

Instep chart from center CDD to end

Instep chart to center CDD

zip line

A **A** **A** **A** **A** **A** **A** **A**
st rpt st rpt st rpt st rpt st rpt st rpt st rpt st rpt

A **A** **A** **A** **A** **A** **A** **A**
st rpt st rpt st rpt st rpt st rpt st rpt st rpt st rpt

second side

toe shaping chart

first side

EOR

BOR

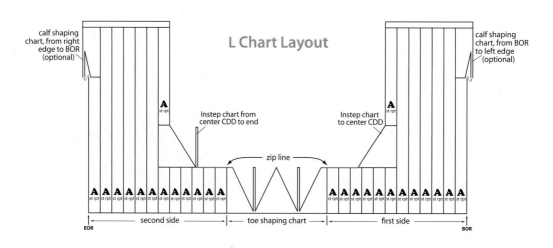

L Chart Layout

calf shaping chart, from right edge to BOR (optional)

calf shaping chart, from BOR to left edge (optional)

A st rpt

A st rpt

Instep chart from center CDD to end

Instep chart to center CDD

zip line

A **A** **A** **A** **A** **A** **A** **A** **A**
st rpt st rpt st rpt st rpt st rpt st rpt st rpt st rpt st rpt

A **A** **A** **A** **A** **A** **A** **A** **A**
st rpt st rpt st rpt st rpt st rpt st rpt st rpt st rpt st rpt

second side

toe shaping chart

first side

EOR

BOR

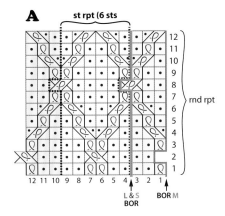

A

st rpt (6 sts)

Note: Use decrease symbols in black and color for your size only.
Treat as blank any squares which contain symbols for other sizes.

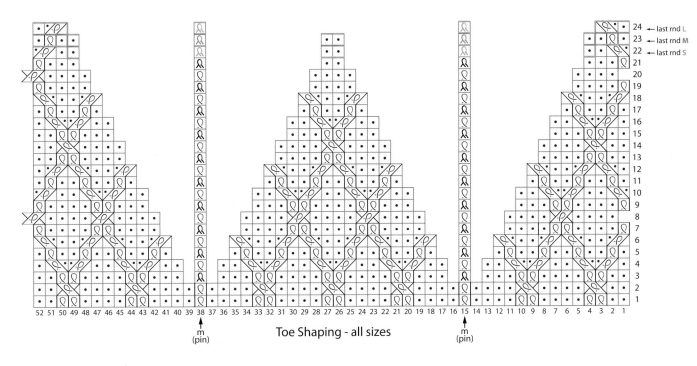

Toe Shaping - all sizes

knit tbl	RC ktbl over ktbl	right extension, chart A (M only, ignore for S & L)
purl	LC ktbl over ktbl	left extension, chart A (M only, ignore for S & L)
(any color) CDD tbl	— end L	for M, treat as unshaded; ignore for S & L
RC ktbl over p	— end M	for M, treat as unshaded; for S & L, RC spans BOR
LC ktbl over p	— end S	LC spans BOR (M only)

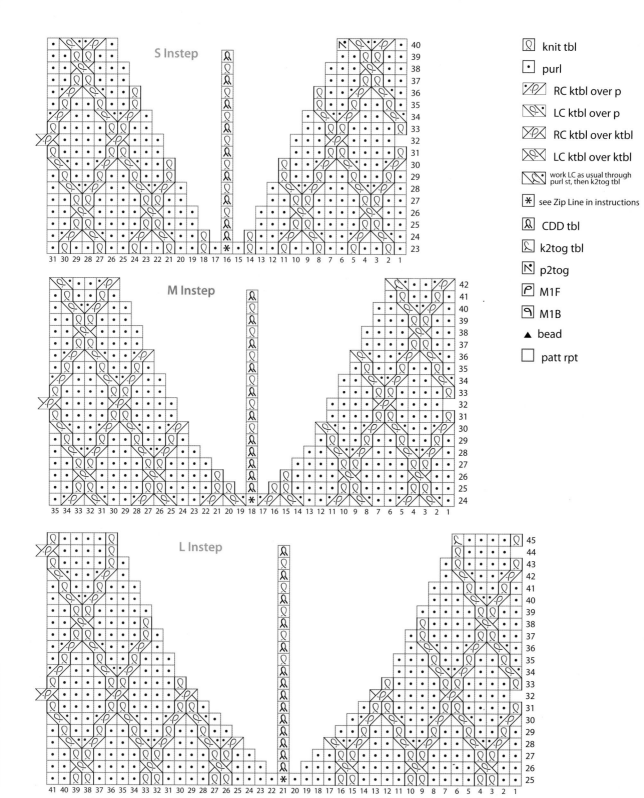

S Instep

M Instep

L Instep

	knit tbl
·	purl
	RC ktbl over p
	LC ktbl over p
	RC ktbl over ktbl
	LC ktbl over ktbl
	work LC as usual through purl st, then k2tog tbl
✳	see Zip Line in instructions
	CDD tbl
	k2tog tbl
	p2tog
	M1F
	M1B
▲	bead
☐	patt rpt

Calf Shaping for size M

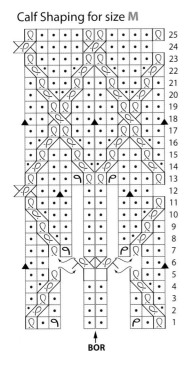

BOR

Calf Shaping for sizes S & L

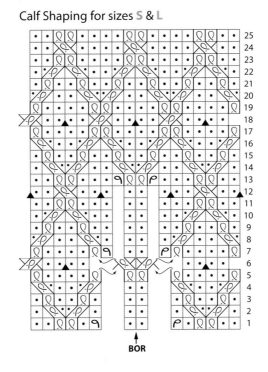

BOR

Ribbing

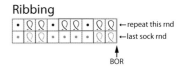

← repeat this rnd
← last sock rnd

BOR

Semi Aran

A common pattern arrangement on Aran-style fisherman's sweaters involves a central panel that is flanked symmetrically by narrower panels, with the narrowest panel used repeatedly as a divider between the other panels. Applying that convention to a sock shape gives opportunities for some of the motifs, purposefully laid out as mirror images, to merge at the center front on the leg or to diverge and multiply for calf shaping. The toe-shaping is especially fun here, because the decrease lines blend right into the pattern motifs and form the centers of two symmetrical bell shapes.

Note
- The vertical repeats of the stitch pattern charts vary, so you will need to move up your round markers for each chart independently. Luckily, once you get the patterns established and a few rounds knitted, the charts will serve mainly to verify that you're reading your knitting correctly.

Yarn
Shown here:
- Madelinetosh Tosh Sock; 100% superwash merino wool; 4.23 oz [120g], 361 meters [395 yds]; 1 (1, 2) skeins Silver Fox (MC)
- Rowan Kidsilk Haze (optional reinforcement for sole); 70% super kid mohair / 30% silk; 0.88 oz [25g], 220 yds [210 meters]; color 634; about 0.28 oz [8g] needed for women's medium

Needles
Change needle size if necessary to get gauge given.
- US size 1½ [2.5mm] — your choice: one long circular at least 40" [100cm], two shorter circulars, or dpns
- one dpn US size 1½ [2.5mm] — not needed if you're already using dpns

Notions
- stitch markers (2 pin-type, 4 any type in 3 colors: c1, c2, c3), tapestry needl

Gauge
- with reinforcing yarn on sole: 32 sts = 4" [10cm], 40 rnds = 4" [10cm]
- without reinforcing yarn, in pattern, unblocked: 40 sts = 4" [10cm], 44 rnds = 4" [10cm]

Size
small (S) - sole about 8.75" [22cm] long, for women's US shoe size 5-6 [Eur size 35/36]
medium (M) - sole about 9.5" [24cm] long, for women's US shoe size 7-8 [Eur size 37/38]
large (L) - sole about 10.25" [26cm] long, for women's US shoe size 9-10 [Eur size 39/40]

Measurements
(lightly blocked)

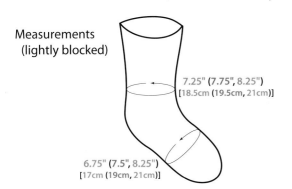

7.25" (7.75", 8.25")
[18.5cm (19.5cm, 21cm)]

6.75" (7.5", 8.25")
[17cm (19cm, 21cm)]

SOLE

Holding MC and reinforcement yarn (optional) together and using a variation of JMCO (page 181), cast on 46 (50, 54) pairs of sts on 2 needle points. Total 92 (100, 108) sts.

Rnd 1 (set-up):
Needle 1: K1, M1F, k1, pm c1 for end of heel, k41 (45, 49), pm c2 for beginning of toe, k3. Needle 2: K1, M1L, k1, pm c2 for end of toe, k41 (45, 49), pm c3 for beginning of heel and BOR (3 sts remain on LN after BOR marker). There are 6 heel sts, 6 toe sts, and 41 (45, 49) sts on each side. Total 94 (102, 110) sts.

Rnds 2 - 12 (14, 16):
Work Sole Heel chart between c3 and c1 markers, k41 (45, 49) side sts, work Sole Toe chart between c2 markers including SRs (page 184) as shown, and k41 (45, 49) side sts. Then k17 (20, 22) to center heel (new BOR for rest of sock). Total 154 (172, 190) sts.

Rnd 13 (15, 17):
Note: This round does not appear on Sole Toe and Sole Heel charts. Removing markers as you go, adjust st count for sock top as follows:
Size S: k17, M1F, (k17, M1F) 7 times, end k18.
Size M: k29, M1F, (k26, M1F) 5 times, end k21.
Size L: k15, k2tog, k156, k2tog, end k15.

Cut reinforcing yarn. Total 162 (178, 188) sts.

FOOT

Toe Shaping

Refer to Chart Layout diagram.
Note: BOR on chart A1 and EOR on chart A2 are the same for all sizes. From center heel BOR with MC, work charts between lines for your size as follows:

Rnd 1 (set-up):
First side: Work chart A1 from BOR, chart B, chart C, chart B, chart A2, chart B, chart C. For **M** & **L** only, work chart B. Total 57 (64, 68) sts.
Toe, all sizes: Work Toe Shaping chart (place markers where indicated). Total 48 (50, 52) sts.
Second side: For **M** & **L** only, work chart B. Then for all sizes, work chart C, chart B, chart A1, chart B, chart C, chart B, and chart A2 to EOR line. Total 57 (64, 68) sts.

Rnds 2 - 21 (22, 23):
First side: Work chart A1 from BOR, chart B, chart C, chart B,

Sole Toe - all sizes

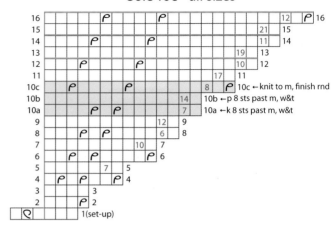

Sole Heel - all sizes

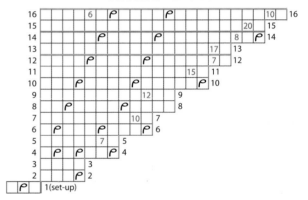

☐ k on RS, p on WS	— end L
P M1F	— end M
R M1L	— end S
☐ short row	| center line
	| **BOR** (beginning of round)

Chart notes:

Brown numbers give stitch counts greater than 5 to next symbol or end of chart.

After set-up round, work each row of chart twice; first from right to left, then from left to right.

OPTIONAL: When working from left to right, use M1B instead of M1F.

chart A2, chart B, chart C. For **M** & **L** only, work chart B.
Toe, all sizes: Work Toe Shaping chart.
Second side: For **M** & **L** only, work chart B. Then for all sizes, work chart C, chart B, chart A1, chart B, chart C, chart B, and chart A2 to EOR line.

Total 118 (134, 144) sts remain.

ZIP LINE
Rnd 22 (23, 24):
Work A1 from BOR, B, C, B, then work to * on Instep chart for your size.
Note: The * represents all sts in the zip line join; they do not appear individually on instep charts.

Join sides of lower foot: Drop working yarn and sl next 12 (15, 17) sts to RN. [If using circular needle(s), don't pull sts on RN to the cable yet.] Sl next 14 (17, 19) sts to dpn (temporary LN). Cut a separate strand of MC about 18" long. Leaving a 4" tail, do k2tog tbl (it twists and leans left) with the separate strand. Slip that st back to LN without turning it. Then make a twisted zip line up the foot with that separate strand by doing the following three steps 11 (14, 16) times:
1. sl 1 st from RN to LN
2. CDD with next 3 sts
3. sl the st just made back to LN, sl it purlwise tbl, return it to LN in its turned position

Then do step 1 again, drop the separate strand, pick up MC working yarn and do last zip CDD tbl with it.

Finish round as follows: Continue to left side of Instep chart, then work charts B, C, B, and A2 to EOR. Total 93 (103, 109) sts remain.

Use a pin to mark center front stitch coming from zip line and position it as first st on LN. It will be the center of instep-shaping CDDs which continue the zip line. See page 179 for handling a CDD that spans a needle intersection.

INSTEP
Rnds 23-39 (24-42, 25-45):
Work A1 from BOR, B, C, B, Instep chart for your size, B, C, B, and A2 to EOR. Total 74 (78, 82) sts remain.

ANKLE
Continue as established using chart lines for your size — chart A1 from BOR, B, C, B, A2 to EOR line, A1 from BOR line, B, C, B, A2 to EOR — until sock measures 5.5" (6", 6.5") [14cm (15cm, 16.5cm)] above sole.

LEG
Decide whether you need calf expansion (see page 179 for options). If not, work as for ankle for about 1.5" (2", 2.5") [4cm (5cm, 6.5cm)] or desired length. End having worked Rnd 8 or 16 of charts A1/A2.

Calf expansion by st increases: Work to end of Rnd 3 of A2.

Rnds 1-37:
Work Calf Shaping chart from BOR, chart B, C, B, A2 to EOR line, A1 from BOR line, B, C, B, and Calf Shaping chart to BOR. Total 86 (90, 94) sts.

End leg here or continue in pattern as established to length desired. End having worked Rnd 8 or 16 of charts A1/A2.

CUFF
Finish socks with cuff of your choice; see page 180 for options. Cuffs shown are 4-st cord BO and 5-st knit & purl cord BO.

FINISHING
Sew in yarn tails on WS, snugging up last st of zip line with tail hanging there.

> "
> Vitality shows not only
> in the ability to persist, but
> in the ability to start over.
> F. Scott Fitzgerald
> "

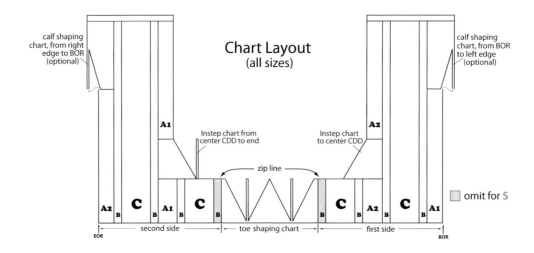

Chart Layout
(all sizes)

calf shaping chart, from right edge to BOR (optional)

A1

Instep chart from center CDD to end

zip line

Instep chart to center CDD

A2

calf shaping chart, from BOR to left edge (optional)

A2 C B A1 C B B B C A2 B C B A1

EOR ← second side → ← toe shaping chart → ← first side → BOR

omit for S

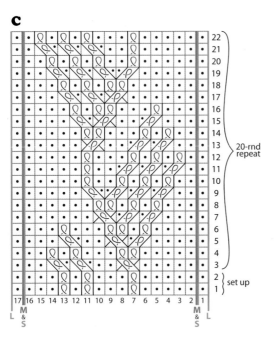

c

22 21 20 19 18 17 16 15 14 13 12 11 10 9 8 7 6 5 4 3 2 1

20-rnd repeat

set up

17 16 15 14 13 12 11 10 9 8 7 6 5 4 3 2 1
L M&S · · · · · M&S L

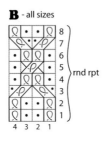

B - all sizes

8 7 6 5 4 3 2 1

rnd rpt

4 3 2 1

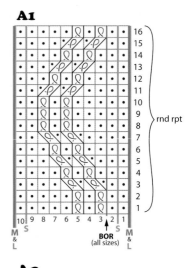

A1

16 15 14 13 12 11 10 9 8 7 6 5 4 3 2 1

rnd rpt

10 9 8 7 6 5 4 3 2 1
M&L S · · · S M&L

BOR (all sizes)

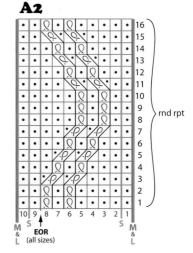

A2

16 15 14 13 12 11 10 9 8 7 6 5 4 3 2 1

rnd rpt

10 9 8 7 6 5 4 3 2 1
M&L S · · · S M&L

EOR (all sizes)

Note: Use decrease symbols in black and color for your size only.
Treat as blank any squares which contain symbols for other sizes.

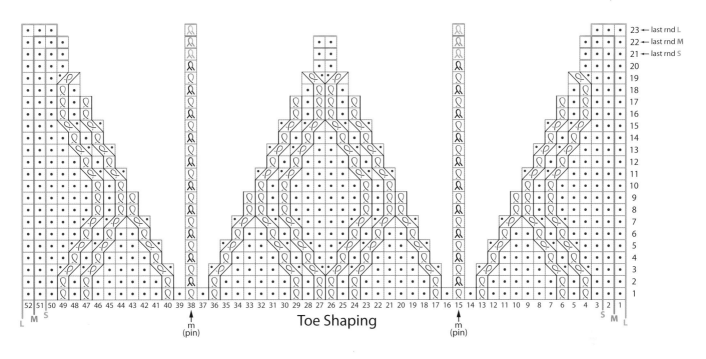

Toe Shaping

| knit tbl |
| purl |
| RC ktbl over p |
| LC ktbl over p |
| RC ktbl over ktbl |
| LC ktbl over ktbl |
| (any color) CDD tbl |
| — end L |
| — end M |
| — end S |

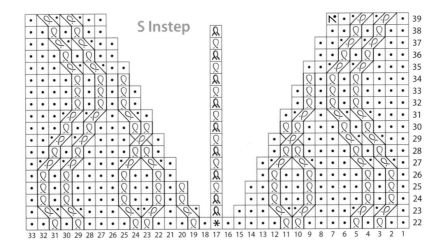

S Instep

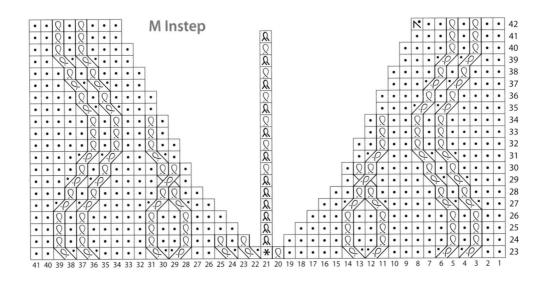

M Instep

⊠	knit tbl	⫫⃗	RC ktbl over p
·	purl	⫤	LC ktbl over p
⊠	p2tog	⫥	RC ktbl over ktbl
⊠	CDD tbl	✳	see Zip Line in instructions
⌐	M1F		
⌐	M1B		

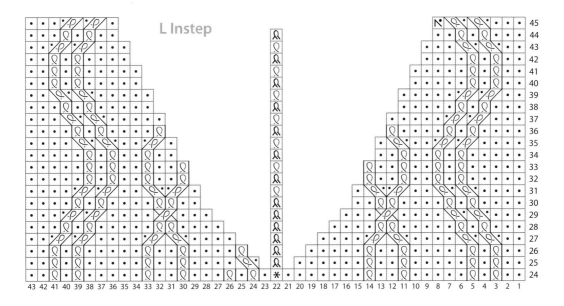

L Instep

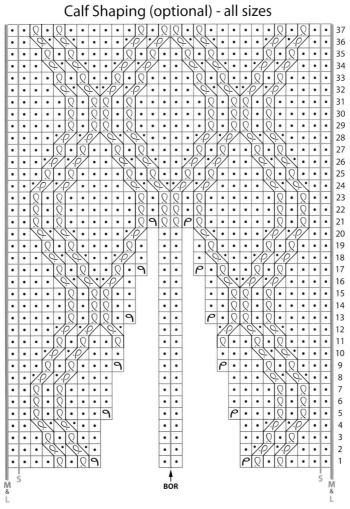

Calf Shaping (optional) - all sizes

Poinsettia

This design evolved from another traveling stitch pattern consisting of concentric diamonds that I had previously devised for socks. I wanted leaves with spines and veins on this one and I wanted the pattern to be simpler, with fewer crosses. On the earlier diamond pattern, every stitch column moved (that is, crossed another stitch) on every other round. None of the lines went straight up at any time. That's a lot of crosses! For this version I straightened the stitch columns on the top half of each inner diamond and presto — leaves. The outer diamonds define the leaf boundaries and a few purl stitches separate them at top and bottom. The upper spines and veins are straight, so you just knit or purl those stitches as they present themselves. Incidentally, you needn't limit yourself to poinsettia colors; the leaf motif makes any leafy color appropriate.

Notes

- Shaping the toe with three lines of centered double decreases every third round fits beautifully with the stitch pattern and makes the toe slightly pointed.
- The structure of this pattern stitch is basically knit 1, purl 1 ribbing. That gives the sock so much elasticity that calf increases will not be needed for most people.
- The cord bind-off cuff will be neater and lie flatter if you knit a plain round before it (the standard way, through the front loops, so the stitches aren't twisted).
- Both sizes have exactly the same number of stitches and rounds; the difference in size is produced by using thinner needles *and thinner yarn* for size M.

Yarn

Shown here:
- *Size L: Blue Moon Socks that Rock;* 100% superwash merino - lightweight; 4.5 oz [127g], 360 yds [329 meters]; 2 skeins Rose Quartz (MC) (note: no reinforcement yarn used on sole of size L sample sock because yarn is relatively thick)
- *Size M: Cascade Yarns Heritage;* 75% Merino Superwash / 25% Nylon; 3.5 oz [100g], 437 yds[400 meters]; 1 skein color 5619 (MC)
- *Rowan Kidsilk Haze (optional reinforcement for sole);* 70% super kid mohair / 30% silk; 0.88 oz [25g], 230 yds [210 meters]; color 661; about 0.28 oz [8g] needed for size **M**.

Needles

Change needle size if necessary to get gauge given.
- **Size L**: US size 1½ [2.5mm] — your choice: one long circular at least 40" [100cm], two shorter circulars, or dpns
- one dpn US size 1½ [2.5mm] — not needed if you're already using dpns
- **Size M**: US size 1½ [2.5mm] for sole with reinforcing yarn — your choice: one long circular at least 40" [100cm], two shorter circulars, or dpns
- US size 1 [2.25mm] for sock top — your choice: one long circular at least 40" [100cm], two shorter circulars, or dpns
- one dpn US size 1 [2.25mm] — not needed if you're already using dpns

Notions

- stitch markers (2 pin-type, 4 any type in 3 colors: c1, c2, c3), tapestry needle

Measurements (lightly blocked)

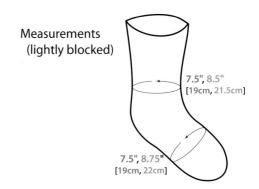

7.5", 8.5" [19cm, 21.5cm]

7.5", 8.75" [19cm, 22cm]

SOLE

Holding MC and reinforcement yarn (optional) together and using a variation of JMCO (page 181), cast on 50 pairs of sts on 2 needle points. Total 100 sts.

Rnd 1 (set-up):

Needle 1: K1, M1F, k1, pm c1 for end of heel, k45, pm c2 for beginning of toe, k3. Needle 2: K1, M1L, k1, pm c2 for end of toe, k45, pm c3 for beginning of heel and BOR (3 sts remain on LN after BOR marker). There are 6 heel sts, 6 toe sts, and 45 sts on each side. Total 102 sts.

Rnds 2-14:

Work Sole Heel chart between c3 and c1 markers, k45 side sts, work Sole Toe chart between c2 markers including SRs (page 184) as shown, and k45 side sts. Then k20 to center heel (new BOR for rest of sock). Total 172 sts.

Rnd 15:

Note: This round does not appear on Sole Toe and Sole Heel charts.

Removing markers as you go, adjust st count for sock top as follows: k23, M1F, (k5, M1F) 25 times, end k24. Cut reinforcing yarn. Total 198 sts.

FOOT
Toe Shaping

Refer to Chart Layout diagram. From center heel BOR with MC and **2.25mm** (2.5mm) needle, work as follows:

Rnd 1 (set-up):

First side: Work chart A 4 times. Total 72 sts.

Toe: Work Toe Shaping chart (place markers where indicated). Total 54 sts.

Second side: Work chart A 4 times. Total 72 sts.

Rnds 2 - 24:

First side: Work chart A 4 times.

Toe: Work Toe Shaping chart.

Second side: Work chart A 4 times.

Total 150 sts remain.

ZIP LINE

Rnd 25:

Work chart A 2 times, then work to * on Instep Shaping chart. Note: The * represents all sts in the zip line join; they do not appear individually on instep charts.

Join sides of lower foot: Drop working yarn and sl next 18 sts to RN. [If using circular needle(s), don't pull sts on RN to the cable yet.] Sl next 19 sts to dpn (temporary LN). Cut a separate strand of MC about 18" long. Slip first st on LN purlwise tbl, return it to LN in its turned position. Leaving a 4" tail, make a twisted zip line up the foot with that separate strand by doing the following three steps 17 times:

1. sl 1 st from RN to LN
2. CDD with next 3 sts
3. sl the st just made back to LN, sl it purlwise tbl, return it to LN in its turned position

Sole Toe

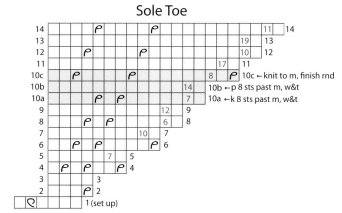

Row	Notes
14	11 14
13	19 13
12	10 12
11	17 11
10c	8 10c ← knit to m, finish rnd
10b	14 10b ← p 8 sts past m, w&t
10a	7 10a ← k 8 sts past m, w&t
9	12 9
8	6 8
7	10 7
6	6
5	7 5
4	4
3	3
2	2
1 (set up)	

Sole Heel

Row	Notes
14	8 14
13	17 13
12	7 12
11	15 11
10	10
9	12 9
8	8
7	10 7
6	6
5	7 5
4	4
3	3
2	2
1 (set up)	

Legend:

- ☐ k MC on RS, p MC on WS
- ℗ M1F
- ℚ M1L
- ☐ short row
- | center line
- | **BOR** (beginning of round)

Chart notes:

Brown numbers give stitch counts greater than 5 to next symbol or end of chart.

After set-up round, work each row of chart twice; first from right to left, then from left to right.

OPTIONAL: When working from left to right, use M1B instead of M1F.

Then do step 1 again, drop the separate strand, pick up MC working yarn and do last zip CDD tbl with it.

Finish round as follows: Continue to left side of Instep chart, then work chart A 2 times. Total 114 sts remain.

Use a pin to mark center front stitch coming from zip line and position it as first st on LN. It will be the center of instep-shaping CDDs. See page 179 for handling a CDD that spans a needle intersection.

INSTEP

Rnds 25-45:
Work chart A 2 times, Instep chart, then chart A 2 times. Total 90 sts remain.

ANKLE

Continue as established — work chart A 5 times on each rnd — until sock measures 6" [15cm] above sole.

LEG

Decide whether you need calf expansion (see page 179 for options). If not, work as for ankle for about 2" [5cm] or desired length. End having worked Rnd 11 or Rnd 23 of chart A.

Calf expansion by st increases: Work to end of Rnd 24 of chart A.

Rnds 1-23:
Work Calf Shaping chart from BOR, chart A 3 times, then Calf Shaping chart to BOR. Total 98 sts.

End leg here or continue in pattern as established to length desired. Last pattern round should be Rnd 11 or Rnd 23 of chart A.

CUFF

Finish socks with cuff of your choice; see page 180 for options. Cuff on pink sock is 4-st cord BO, preceded by one round of knit tfl. On the red sock, the cuff is facing with picot edge, preceded by the following rnd:

Set-up rnd:
K3, k2tog, (k4, k2tog) as many times as will fit. Knit to end of rnd.

FINISHING

Sew in yarn tails on WS, snugging up last st of zip line with tail hanging there.

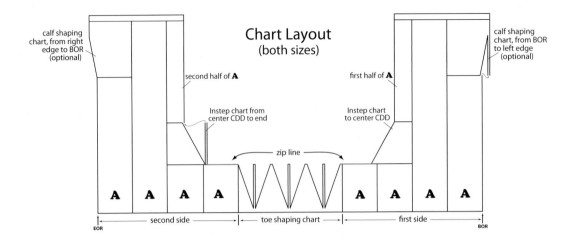

Chart Layout
(both sizes)

Legend:

⊠ knit tbl		⧄ RC ktbl over p	
⊡ purl		⧅ LC ktbl over p	
⊠ CDD tbl		✳ see Zip Line in instructions	

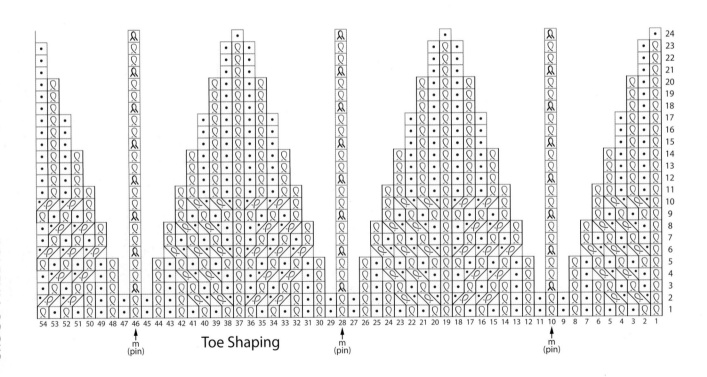

Toe Shaping

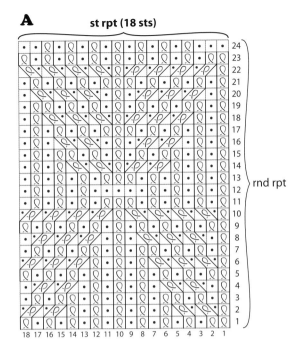

A

st rpt (18 sts)

rnd rpt

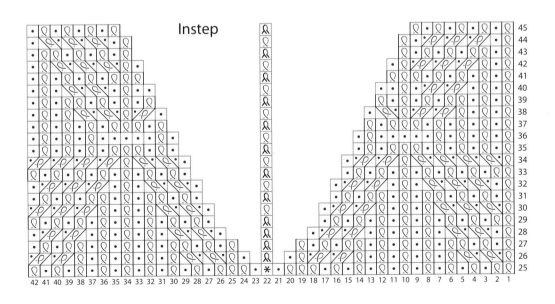

Instep

Calf Shaping

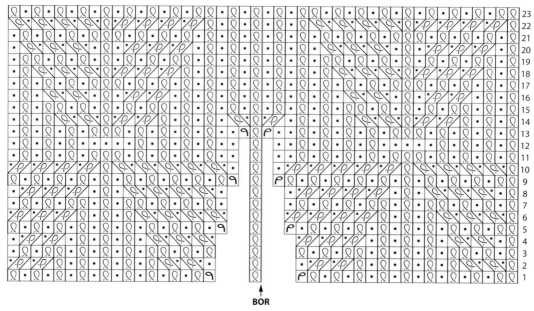

⟨Q⟩ knit tbl

⟨•⟩ purl

⟨╱Q╱⟩ RC ktbl over p

⟨╲Q╲⟩ LC ktbl over p

⟨P⟩ M1F

⟨٩⟩ M1B

> "
> ## An expert is a person who has made all the mistakes that can be made in a very narrow field.
>
> Niels Bohr
>
> "

LACE

Lace Trellis

Here's the fourth version of our familiar diamond-trellis motif, in lace this time. The two lines of centered double decreases that shape the toe are placed where lines of yarn-overs would fall in the pattern. This both preserves the trellis pattern around the toe and strengthens the toe. The trellis lines are all staidly straight when the sock is lying flat, but when it is worn the long lines closest to the instep transform into graceful, symmetrical curves on each side of the center front.

Measurements
(lightly blocked)

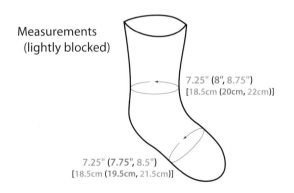

7.25" (8", 8.75")
[18.5cm (20cm, 22cm)]

7.25" (7.75", 8.5")
[18.5cm (19.5cm, 21.5cm)]

Notes
- The plain stockinette section at the back of the heel is triangular, allowing it to coordinate with the stitch pattern. You can use Long Heel Stitch on this section (page 182) to further strengthen the heel if you like.

Yarn
Shown here:
- ***Miss Babs "Yummy" Monochrome Sock & Baby yarn;*** 2-ply Superwash 100% Merino Wool; 4 oz [113 g], 400 yds [365 meters]; 1 (1, 2) skeins Aubergine (MC)
- ***Schulana Kid Seta (optional reinforcement for sole);*** 70% super kid mohair / 30% silk; 0.88 oz [25g], 230 yds [210 meters]; color 22; about 0.28 oz [8g] needed for women's medium

Needles
Change needle size if necessary to get gauge given.
- US size 1½ [2.5mm] — your choice: one long circular at least 40" [100cm], two shorter circulars, or dpns
- one dpn US size 1½ [2.5mm] — not needed if you're already using dpns

Notions
- stitch markers (2 pin-type, 4 any type in 3 colors: c1, c2, c3), tapestry needle

Gauge
- with reinforcing yarn on sole: 32 sts = 4" [10cm], 40 rnds = 4" [10cm]
- without reinforcing yarn, in pattern, unblocked: 30 sts = 4" [10cm], 42 rnds = 4" [10cm]

Size
small (S) - sole about 8.75" [22cm] long, for women's US shoe size 5-6 [Eur size 35/36]

medium (M) - sole about 9.5" [24cm] long, for women's US shoe size 7-8 [Eur size 37/38]

large (L) - sole about 10.25" [26cm] long, for women's US shoe size 9-10 [Eur size 39/40]

SOLE

Holding MC and reinforcement yarn (optional) together and using a variation of JMCO (page 181), cast on 44 (47, 51) pairs of sts on 2 needle points. Total 88 (94, 102) sts.

Rnd 1 (set-up):

Needle 1: K1, M1F, k1, pm c1 for end of heel, k39 (42, 46), pm c2 for beginning of toe, k3. Needle 2: K1, M1L, k1, pm c2 for end of toe, k39 (42, 46), pm c3 for beginning of heel and BOR (3 sts remain on LN following BOR marker). There are 6 heel sts, 6 toe sts, and 39 (42, 46) sts on each side. Total 90 (96, 104) sts.

Rnds 2 - 12 (14, 16):

Work Sole Heel chart between c3 and c1 markers, k39 (42, 46) side sts, work Sole Toe chart between c2 markers including SRs (page 184) as shown, and k39 (42, 46) side sts. Then k15 (17, 20) to center heel (new BOR for rest of sock). Total 142 (156, 174) sts.

Rnd 13 (15, 17):

Note: This round does not appear on Sole Toe and Sole Heel charts.

Removing markers as you go, adjust st count for sock top as follows:

Size S: k47, M1F, k48, M1F, end k47.
Size M: Knit (no adjustment needed).
Size L: k13, k2tog, (k27, k2tog) 5 times, end k14.

Cut reinforcing yarn. Total 144 (156, 168) sts.

FOOT

Toe Shaping

Refer to Chart Layout diagram for your size. From center heel BOR with MC, work as follows:

Set-up Rnd:

First side: Work Back Heel chart from BOR, then chart A st rpt 4 (5, 6) times. Total 48 (54, 60) sts.
Toe, all sizes: Work Toe Shaping chart (place markers where indicated). Total 54 sts.
Second side: Work chart A st rpt 3 (4, 5) times, then Back Heel chart to BOR. Total 42 (48, 54) sts.

Rnds 1 - 22 (23, 24):

First side: Work Back Heel chart from BOR, then chart A st rpt 5 (6, 7) times.
Toe, all sizes: Work Toe Shaping chart.

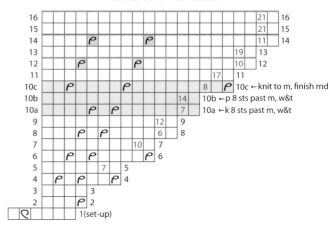

Sole Toe - all sizes

10c ← knit to m, finish rnd
10b ← p 8 sts past m, w&t
10a ← k 8 sts past m, w&t

1(set-up)

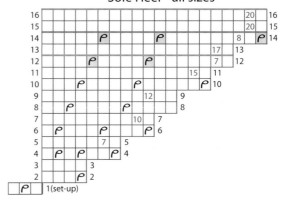

Sole Heel - all sizes

1(set-up)

☐ k on RS, p on WS
℗ M1F
℟ M1L
| center line
| **BOR** (beginning of round)

— end L
— end M
— end S

▨ for size M only omit increases
▨ for size S only omit increases
▨ short row

Chart notes:

Brown numbers give stitch counts greater than 5 to next symbol or end of chart.

After set-up round, work each row of chart twice; first from right to left, then from left to right.

OPTIONAL: When working from left to right, use M1B instead of M1F.

Second side: Work chart A st rpt 4 (5, 6) times, then Back Heel chart to BOR.

Total 97 (109, 121) sts remain.

ZIP LINE

Rnd 23 (24, 25):
Work Back Heel chart from BOR, chart A st rpt 1 (2, 2) times, then to * on Instep chart for your size.
Note: The * represents all sts in the zip line join; they do not appear individually on instep charts.

Join sides of lower foot: Drop working yarn and sl next 10 (12,14) sts to RN. [If using circular needle(s), don't pull RN cable through sts yet.] Sl next 12 (14,16) sts to dpn (temporary LN). Cut a separate strand of MC about 18" long. Leaving a 4" tail, k2tog with the separate strand. Slip that st back to LN without turning it. Then make a zip line up the foot with that separate strand by doing the following three steps 9 (11, 13) times:
1. sl 1 st from RN to LN
2. CDD with next 3 sts
3. sl st just made back to LN

Then do step 1 again, drop the separate strand, pick up MC working yarn and do last zip CDD with it.

Finish round as follows: Continue to left side of Instep chart, work chart A st rpt 1 (1, 2) times, then Back Heel chart to BOR. Total 76 (84, 92) sts remain.

Use a pin to mark center front stitch coming from zip line and position it as first st on LN. It will be the center of instep-shaping CDDs. See page 179 for handling a CDD that spans a needle intersection.

INSTEP

Rnds 24 (25, 26) - 30 (end of Back Heel chart):
Work Back Heel chart from BOR, chart A st rpt 1 (2, 2) times, Instep chart for your size, chart A st rpt 1 (1, 2) times, then to BOR of Back Heel chart. Total 64 (72, 82) sts.
Note: When a decrease spans BOR, sl first st of rnd, work to 1 st before end of rnd, then work decrease using first and last sts of rnd.

Rnds 31-40 (42, 44):
Work chart A st rpt 4 (5, 5) times, Instep chart for your size, and chart A st rpt 4 (4, 5) times. Total 54 (60, 66) sts remain.

ANKLE

Work chart A st rpt 9 (10, 11) times on each rnd until sock measures 5.5" (6", 6.5") [14cm (15cm, 16.5cm)] above sole.

LEG

Decide whether you need calf expansion (see page 179 for options). If not, work as for ankle for about 1.5" (2", 2.5") [4cm (5cm, 6.5cm)] or desired length. End having worked Rnd 1 or 7 of chart A.

Calf expansion by st increases: Work to end of Rnd 12 of chart A.

Rnds 1-25:
Work from BOR of Calf Shaping chart, chart A st rpt 7 (8, 9) times, then Calf Shaping chart to BOR. For a 6-st increase, stop at the end of Rnd 13, or to increase 12 sts continue through Rnd 25. Total 60 (66, 72) sts or 66 (72, 78) sts.

End leg here or continue in pattern to length desired. End having worked Rnd 1 or 7 of chart A.

CUFF

Finish socks with cuff of your choice; see page 180 for options. Cuffs shown are 4-st cord BO and 8 rnds of half-twisted ribbing.

FINISHING

Sew in yarn tails on WS, snugging up last st of zip line with tail hanging there.

> " Don't make the same mistake twice or you'll never get around to all of them.
>
> unknown
>
> "

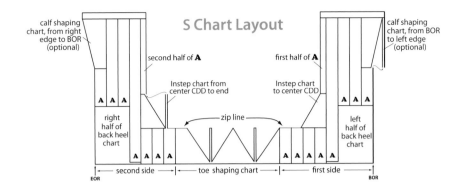

S Chart Layout

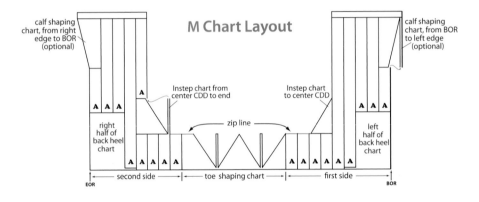

M Chart Layout

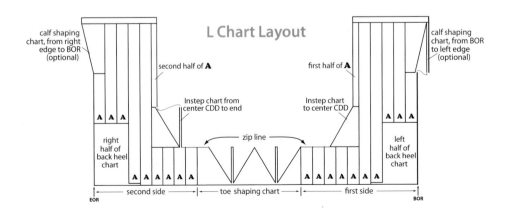

L Chart Layout

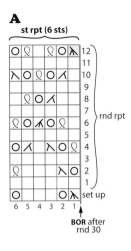

A

st rpt (6 sts)

set up

BOR after
rnd 30

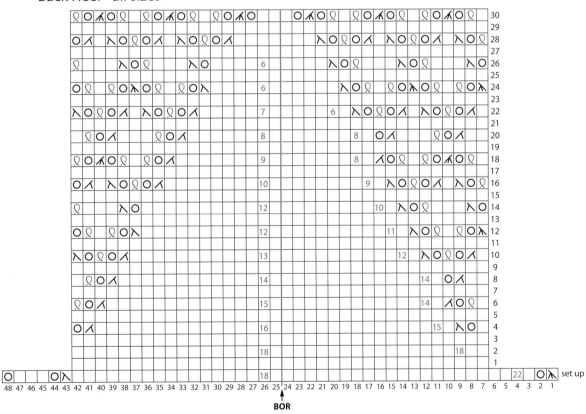

on rnds 36, 48, 60, 72, 84,
& 96 at BOR only: sl first 2 sts
of rnd, work to last st, do
Sk2togP as first st of next rnd

☐ knit   ↗ sskSPS

○ YO   ↘ Sk2togP

↗ k2tog   ℚ k tbl

↘ ssk

Back Heel - all sizes

LACE TRELLIS

Note: Use decrease symbols in black and color for your size only.
Treat as blank any squares which contain symbols for other sizes.

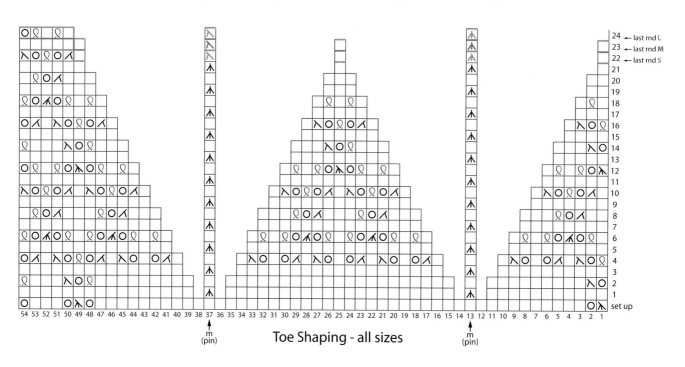

Toe Shaping - all sizes

Calf Shaping - all sizes

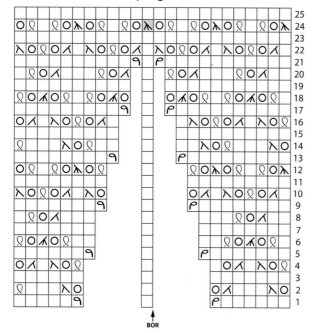

⋏ sl first 2 sts of rnd, work to last
st, do Sk2togP as first st of next rnd

☐ knit   ⋏ (any color) CDD

⊘ YO   ⋉ (any color) ssk

⋏ k2tog   ⋉ sskSPS

⊘ k tbl   ⋏ Sk2togP

ℙ M1F   — end L

ℚ M1B   — end M

✳ see Zip Line   — end S
   in instructions

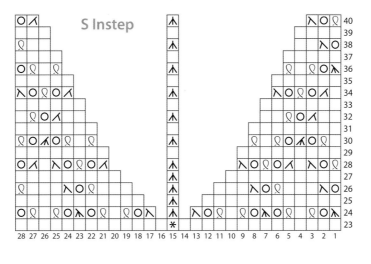

S Instep

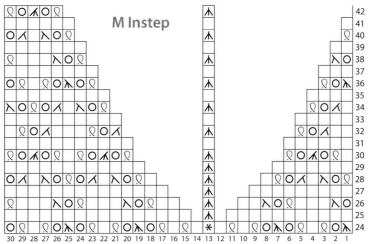

M Instep

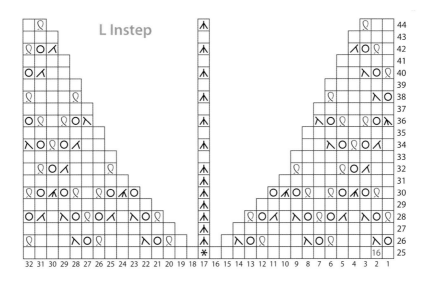

L Instep

Meandering Mesh

Distraction is another way to deal with the natural horizontal color lines and pooling of variegated yarn. In this design, the diagonal lace panels lead the eye up at an angle to the left, while the right-leaning decreases in the lace lead its stitch columns up to the right. The mesh panels would also have been effective mirror-imaged from side to side, with axes of symmetry at the center front and back. However, I decided that those lines of mesh meandered in a more interesting way on the lower foot when they all leaned to the left. Then, when they get to the leg, they politely stop meandering and settle into orderly spirals.

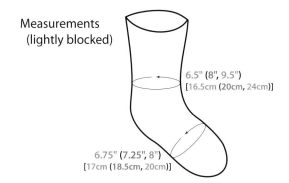

Measurements
(lightly blocked)

6.5" (8", 9.5")
[16.5cm (20cm, 24cm)]

6.75" (7.25", 8")
[17cm (18.5cm, 20cm)]

Notes

- If you elect to reinforce the heel with Long Heel Stitch, you'll want to use markers to indicate where it begins and ends.
- The M1LO (make 1 by lift only; see toe-shaping charts) helps to maintain integrity of the two mesh diagonals as they merge on the toe. When followed or preceded by a yarn-over, this increase allows two separate lace holes to be made side by side.

Yarn

Shown here:
- *Regia 4-ply Design Line;* 75% superwash new wool / 25% polyamide; 1.75 oz [50g], 230 yds [210 meters]; 1 (1, 1) ball color 04260 (MC)
- *Regia 4-ply;* 75% superwash new wool / 25% polyamide; 1.75 oz [50g], 230 yds [210 meters]; 1 (1, 1) ball color 00540 (CC)
- *Schulana Kid Seta (optional reinforcement for sole);* 70% super kid mohair / 30% silk; 0.88 oz [25g], 230 yds [210 meters]; color 22; about 0.28 oz [8g] needed for women's medium

Needles

Change needle size if necessary to get gauge given.
- US size 1 US size 1½ [2.5mm] for sole with reinforcing yarn — your choice: one long circular at least 40" [100cm], two shorter circulars, or dpns
- US size 1 [2.25mm] for sock top — your choice: one long circular at least 40" [100cm], two shorter circulars, or dpns
- one dpn US size 1 [2.25mm] — not needed if you're already using dpns

Notions

- stitch markers (2 pin-type, 4 any type in 3 colors: c1, c2, c3), tapestry needle

Gauge

- with reinforcing yarn on sole: 32 sts = 4" [10cm], 40 rnds = 4" [10cm]
- without reinforcing yarn, in pattern, unblocked: 30 sts = 4" [10cm], 46 rnds = 4" [10cm]

Size

small (S) - sole about 8.75" [22cm] long, for women's US shoe size 5-6 [Eur size 35/36]

medium (M) - sole about 9.5" [24cm] long, for women's US shoe size 7-8 [Eur size 37/38]

large (L) - sole about 10.25" [26cm] long, for women's US shoe size 9-10 [Eur size 39/40]

SOLE

Holding CC and reinforcement yarn (optional) together and using a variation of JMCO (page 181), cast on 46 (49, 54) pairs of sts on 2 needle points. Total 92 (98, 108) sts.

Rnd 1 (set-up):
Needle 1: K1, M1F, k1, pm c1 for end of heel, k41 (44, 49), pm c2 for beginning of toe, k3. Needle 2: K1, M1L, k1, pm c2 for end of toe, k41 (44, 49), pm c3 for beginning of heel and BOR (3 sts remain on LN after BOR marker). There are 6 heel sts, 6 toe sts, and 41 (44, 49) sts on each side. Total 94 (100, 110) sts.

Rnds 2-12 (14, 16):
Work Sole Heel chart between c3 and c1 markers, k41 (44, 49) side sts, work Sole Toe chart between c2 markers including SRs (page 184) as shown, and k41 (44, 49) side sts. Then k15 (17, 20) to center heel (new BOR for rest of sock). Total 146 (160, 180) sts.

Rnd 13 (15, 17):
Note: This round does not appear on Sole Toe and Sole Heel charts.

Removing markers as you go, adjust st count for sock top as follows:
Size S: Knit (no adjustment needed).
Size M: k50, M1F, k60, M1F, end k50 .
Size L: k10, k2tog, k156, k2tog, end k10.

Cut yarn(s). Total 146 (162, 178) sts.

FOOT

Toe Shaping
Refer to Chart Layout diagram for your size. From center heel BOR with MC and 2.25mm needle, work as follows:

Rnd 1 (set-up):
First side: Work st rpt of Long Heel Stitch chart 6 times, from start line for your size on chart A1 to end of st rpt, then chart A1 st rpt 2 (2, 3) times more. Total 48 (54, 60) sts.
Toe: Work Toe Shaping chart for your size (place markers where indicated). Total 50 (54, 58) sts.
Second side: Work st rpt of chart A1 3 (3, 4) times. For size M only, work the 6-st left extension of chart A1. For all sizes, work st rpt of Long Heel Stitch chart 6 times. Total 48 (54, 60) sts.

Rnds 2 - 21 (22, 23):
First side: Work st rpt of Long Heel Stitch chart 6 times, from start

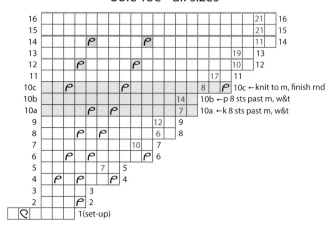

Sole Toe - all sizes

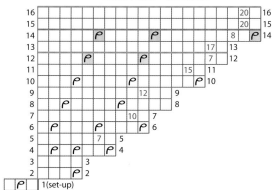

Sole Heel - all sizes

☐ k on RS, p on WS	— end L	
℗ M1F	— end M	
℧ M1L	— end S	
│ center line	▨ for size M only omit increases	
┃ BOR (beginning of round)	▨ for size S only omit increases	
	☐ short row	

Chart notes:
Brown numbers give stitch counts greater than 5 to next symbol or end of chart.

After set-up round, work each row of chart twice; first from right to left, then from left to right.

OPTIONAL: When working from left to right, use M1B instead of M1F.

SOLEFULL SOCKS

line for your size on chart A1 to end of st rpt, then chart A1 st rpt 2 (2, 3) times more.

Toe: Work Toe Shaping chart for your size.

Second side: Work st rpt of chart A1 3 (3, 4) times. For size M only, work the 6-st left extension of chart A1. For all sizes, work st rpt of Long Heel Stitch chart 6 times.

Total 104 (120, 136) sts remain.

ZIP LINE
Rnd 22 (23, 24):
Work st rpt of Long Heel Stitch chart 6 times, from start line for your size on chart A1 to end of st rpt, chart A1 st rpt 0 (0, 1) times more, then work to * on Instep chart for your size.

Note: The * represents all sts in the zip line join; they do not appear individually on instep charts.

Join sides of lower foot: Join the two sides of lower foot as follows: Drop working yarn and sl next 11 (12, 14) sts to RN. [If using circular needle(s), don't pull sts on RN to the cable yet.] Sl next 13 (14, 16) sts to dpn (temporary LN). Cut a separate strand of MC about 18" long. Leaving a 4" tail, k2tog with the separate strand. Slip that st back to LN without turning it. Then make a zip line up the foot with that separate strand by doing the following three steps 10 (11, 13) times:
1. sl 1 st from RN to LN
2. CDD with next 3 sts
3. sl st just made back to LN

Then do step 1 again, drop the separate strand, pick up MC working yarn and do last zip CDD with it.

Finish round as follows: Continue to left side of Instep chart, then st rpt of chart A1 1 (1, 2) times. For size M only, work the 6-st left extension of chart A1. For all sizes, work st rpt of Long Heel Stitch chart 6 times. Total 81 (95, 107) sts remain.

Use a pin to mark center front stitch coming from zip line and position it as first st on LN. It will be the center of instep-shaping CDDs. See page 179 for handling a CDD that spans a needle intersection.

INSTEP
Rnds 23 (24, 25) - 30 (end of chart A1 and Long Heel Stitch chart):
Work st rpt of Long Heel Stitch chart 6 times, from start line for your size on chart A1 to end of st rpt, chart A1 st rpt 0 (0, 1) times more, Instep chart for your size, then st rpt of chart A1 1 (1, 2) times. For size M only, work the 6-st left extension of chart A1. For all sizes, work st rpt of Long Heel Stitch chart 6 times. Total 65 (81, 95) sts remain.

Rnds 31-43 (47, 51):
Work from BOR for your size on chart A2 to end of st rpt, chart A2 st rpt 1 (1, 2) times more, Instep chart for your size, then st rpt of chart A2 2 (2, 3) times. For size M only, work the 6-st left extension of chart A2. Total 48 (60, 72) sts remain.

ANKLE
Continue as established — on each rnd work from BOR for your size on chart A2 to end of st rpt, then chart A2 st rpt 3 (3, 5) times more; for size M only, work the 6-st left extension of chart A2 — until sock measures 5.5" (6", 6.5") [14cm (15cm, 16.5cm)] above sole.

LEG
Decide whether you need calf expansion (see page 179 for options). If not, work as for ankle for about 1.5" (2", 2.5") [4cm (5cm, 6.5cm)] or desired length.

Calf expansion by st increases: Continue in pattern but increase one stitch at symmetrical places on each side of center back about every 4th round. Mirror them if you like, such as M1F on righthand side of center back and M1B on lefthand side. Make as many or as few increases as desired, but keep them mostly on the back half of the sock. It's helpful to mark the increases with a pin after you make them, to keep track of how many extra stitches each area has.

After the calf increases, continue to maintain stitch pattern to length desired. Knit one rnd in CC.

CUFF
Finish socks with cuff of your choice in CC; see page 180 for options. One cuff shown is 4-st cord BO and the other is facing with picot edge.

FINISHING
Sew in yarn tails on WS, snugging up last st of zip line with tail hanging there.

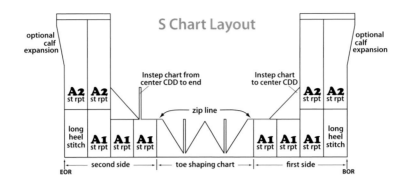

S Chart Layout

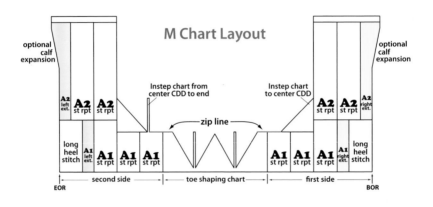

M Chart Layout

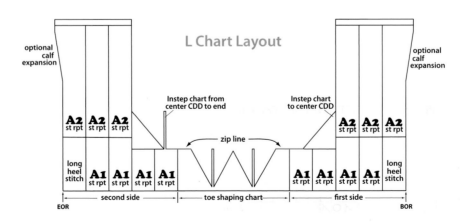

L Chart Layout

A2 (after rnd 30)

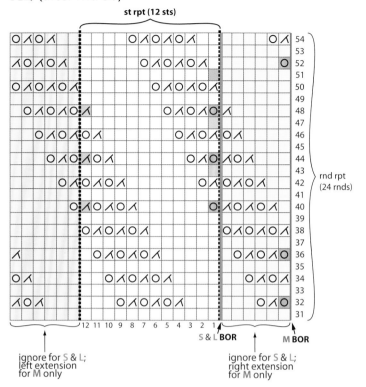

st rpt (12 sts)

rnd rpt (24 rnds)

12 11 10 9 8 7 6 5 4 3 2 1

S & L **BOR**   **M BOR**

ignore for S & L;
left extension
for M only

ignore for S & L;
right extension
for M only

A1 (rnds 1-30 only)

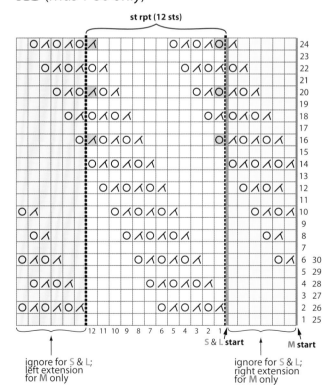

st rpt (12 sts)

12 11 10 9 8 7 6 5 4 3 2 1

S & L **start**   **M start**

ignore for S & L;
left extension
for M only

ignore for S & L;
right extension
for M only

☐ knit

◺ k2tog

◯ YO

☐ right extension, charts A1 & A2

☐ left extension, charts A1 & A2

▨ ignore for M and L;
do as shown at square
of this color on
S Instep chart rnd 43

☐ ignore for S and L;
do as shown at square
of this color on
M Instep chart rnd 47

▨ ignore for S and M;
do as shown at square
of this color on
L Instep chart rnd 51

◉ **on A2 at BOR only:** reposition first st of rnd
to same needle (or cable) as last st of rnd
(it will be used in k2tog at end of rnd),
then do YO (becomes first st of rnd)

◸ **on A2 at needle intersection only:** sl last
st on RN to LN, k2tog, sl st just made back
to righthand side of needle intersection

◺ or ◉ **on A1:** for M, always k2tog or YO as
shown; for S & L, treat as blank
when these squares are adjacent
to heel area

⑨ knit, wrapping twice

Ⅴ sl wyib

Long Heel Stitch
(optional)

2-st rpt

| Ⅴ | | 2 | ⎫ 2-rnd rpt |
| ⑨ | | 1 | ⎭ |

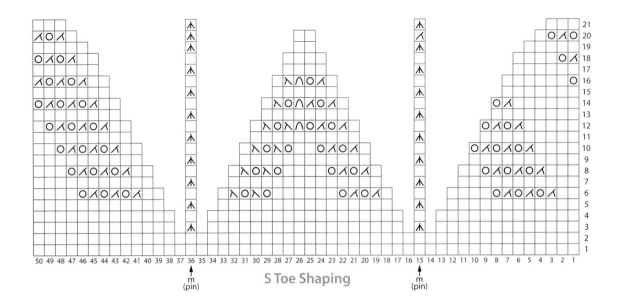

S Toe Shaping

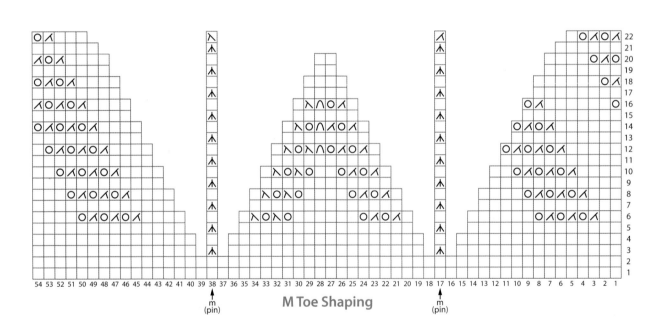

M Toe Shaping

□ knit   ∧ M1LO (lift only)

⟋ k2tog   O YO

⟍ ssk   ⋏ CDD

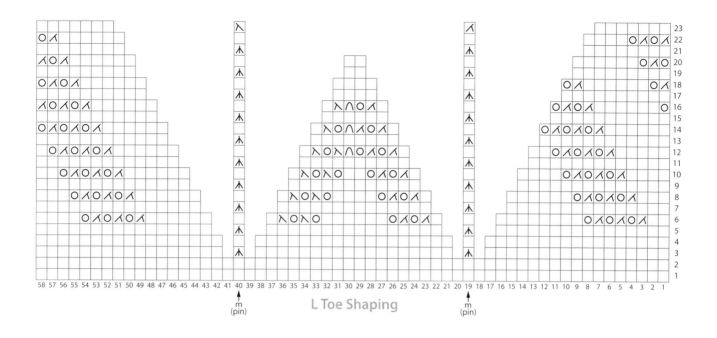

L Toe Shaping

“

The greater danger for most
of us lies not in setting our aim
too high and falling short; but
in setting our aim too low,
and achieving our mark.

Michelangelo Buonarroti

”

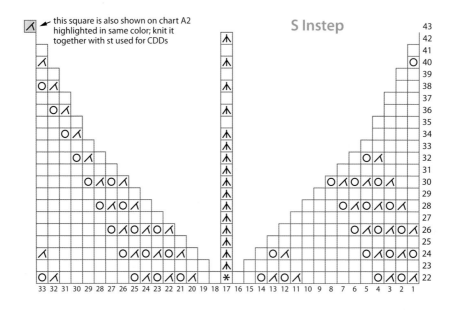

this square is also shown on chart A2 highlighted in same color; knit it together with st used for CDDs

S Instep

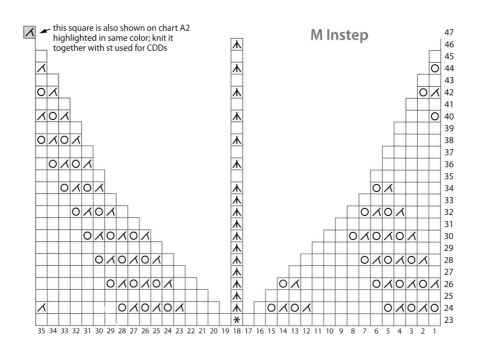

this square is also shown on chart A2 highlighted in same color; knit it together with st used for CDDs

M Instep

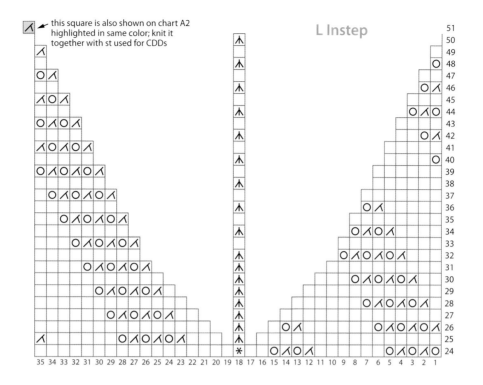

this square is also shown on chart A2 highlighted in same color; knit it together with st used for CDDs

L Instep

☐ knit	⋏ CDD
⟋ k2tog	✳ see Zip Line in instructions
⊙ YO	

Twining Vines

The mirror imaging of these vines at the center front and back makes for interesting convergences and satisfying symmetry. If you hold the finished and blocked sock up to the light, the lace holes on each side line up perfectly with each other. The single-stitch column between pattern repeats is a chameleon: it undulates gracefully on the sock sides, then magically straightens up at the center front and back because of the mirror imaging.

Measurements
(lightly blocked)

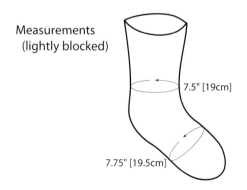

7.5" [19cm]

7.75" [19.5cm]

Notes
- Variegated yarn with low-contrast colors would be interesting in this design, because the horizontal color lines would bend gently into alternating diagonals. On the other hand, high-contrast colors would obscure the vines.
- The stitch pattern is "Vine Lace Zigzag" from Barbara Walker's *A Treasury of Knitting Patterns* (often called her first treasury).

Yarn
Shown here:
- *Miss Babs "Yummy" Monochrome Sock & Baby yarn;* 2-ply Superwash 100% Merino Wool; 4 oz [113 g], 400 yds [365 meters]; 1 (1, 2) skeins Verdigris (MC)
- *Rowan Kidsilk Haze (optional reinforcement for sole);* 70% super kid mohair / 30% silk; 0.88 oz [25g], 230 yds [210 meters]; color 629; about 0.28 oz [8g] needed for women's medium

Needles
Change needle size if necessary to get gauge given.
- US size 1½ [2.5mm] — your choice: one long circular at least 40" [100cm], two shorter circulars, or dpns
- one dpn US size 1½ [2.5mm] — not needed if you're already using dpns

Notions
- stitch markers (2 pin-type, 4 any type in 3 colors: c1, c2, c3), tapestry needle

Gauge
- with reinforcing yarn on sole: 32 sts = 4" [10cm], 40 rnds = 4" [10cm]
- without reinforcing yarn, in pattern, unblocked: 35 sts = 4" [10cm], 42 rnds = 4" [10cm]

Size
medium - sole about 9.5" [24cm] long, for women's US shoe size 7-8 [Eur size 37/38]

SOLE

Holding MC and reinforcement yarn (optional) together and using a variation of JMCO (page 181), cast on 49 pairs of sts on 2 needle points. Total 98 sts.

Rnd 1 (set-up):

Needle 1: K1, M1F, k1, pm c1 for end of heel, k44, pm c2 for beginning of toe, k3. Needle 2: K1, M1L, k1, pm c2 for end of toe, k44, pm c3 for beginning of heel and BOR (3 sts remain on LN after BOR marker). There are 6 heel sts, 6 toe sts, and 44 sts on each side. Total 100 sts.

Rnds 2-14:

Work Sole Heel chart between c3 and c1 markers, k44 side sts, work Sole Toe chart between c2 markers including SRs (page 184) as shown, and k44 side sts. Then k17 to center heel (new BOR for rest of sock). Total 164 sts.

Rnd 15:

Note: This round does not appear on Sole Toe and Sole Heel charts.

Removing markers as you go, adjust st count for sock top as follows: k13, k2tog, (k25, k2tog) 5 times, end k14. Total 158 sts.

FOOT
Toe Shaping

Refer to Chart Layout diagram. From center heel BOR with MC, work as follows:

Rnd 1 (set-up):

First side: Work st rpt of Long Heel Stitch chart 5 times, on to end of Long Heel Stitch chart [11 heel sts], then chart A 4 times. Total 55 sts.

Toe: Work Toe Shaping chart (place markers where indicated). Total 48 sts.

Second side: Work chart B 4 times, from beginning of Long Heel Stitch chart through st rpt, then st rpt of Long Heel Stitch chart 4 times [11 heel sts]. Total 55 sts.

Rnds 2 - 23:

First side: Work st rpt of Long Heel Stitch chart 5 times, on to end of Long Heel Stitch chart, chart A 4 times.

Toe, all sizes: Work Toe Shaping chart.

Second side: Work chart B 4 times, from beginning of Long Heel Stitch chart through st rpt, then st rpt of Long Heel Stitch chart 4 times.

Total 114 sts remain.

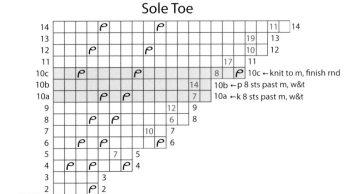

Sole Toe

10c ←knit to m, finish rnd
10b ←p 8 sts past m, w&t
10a ←k 8 sts past m, w&t

1 (set up)

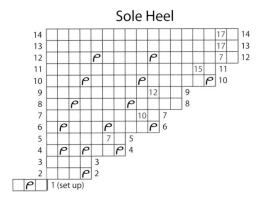

Sole Heel

1 (set up)

☐ k MC on RS, p MC on WS

🄿 M1F

🅀 M1L

▨ short row

❘ center line

❘ **BOR** (beginning of round)

Chart notes:

Brown numbers give stitch counts greater than 5 to next symbol or end of chart.

After set-up round, work each row of chart twice; first from right to left, then from left to right.

OPTIONAL: When working from left to right, use M1B instead of M1F.

ZIP LINE

Rnd 24:

Work st rpt of Long Heel Stitch chart 5 times, on to end of Long Heel Stitch chart, chart A 2 times, then work to * on Instep chart. Note: The * represents all sts in the zip line join; they do not appear individually on Instep chart.

Join sides of lower foot: Drop working yarn and sl next 11 sts to RN. [If using circular needle(s), don't pull sts on RN to the cable yet.] Sl next 14 sts to dpn (temporary LN). Cut a separate strand of MC about 18" long. Work as follows with that separate strand: leaving a 4" tail, sl 1 knitwise, k2tog, psso. Slip that st back to LN without turning it. Then make a zip line up the foot by doing the following three steps 10 times:

1. sl 1 st from RN to LN
2. CDD with next 3 sts
3. sl st just made back to LN

Then do step 1 again, drop the separate strand, pick up MC working yarn and do last zip CDD with it.

Finish rnd as follows: Continue to left side of Instep chart, chart B once, from beginning of Long Heel Stitch chart through st rpt, then st rpt of Long Heel Stitch chart 4 times. Total 90 sts remain.

Use a pin to mark center front stitch coming from zip line and position it as first st on LN. It will be the center of instep-shaping CDDs. See page 179 for handling a CDD that spans a needle intersection.

INSTEP

Rnds 25-30:

Work st rpt of Long Heel Stitch chart 5 times, on to end of Long Heel Stitch chart, chart A 2 times, Instep chart, chart B once, from beginning of Long Heel Stitch chart through st rpt, then st rpt of Long Heel Stitch chart 4 times. Total 78 sts remain.

Rnds 30-42:

Work chart A 3 times, Instep chart, chart B 2 times. Total 66 sts remain.

ANKLE

Continue as established — work chart A 3 times and chart B 3 times on each rnd — until sock measures 6" [15cm] above sole.

LEG

Decide whether you need calf expansion (see page 179 for options). If not, work as for ankle for about 2" [5cm] or desired length. For best design balance, end having worked a Rnd 3 or 13 of charts A and B.

Calf expansion by st increases, Rnds 64-93: Work to end of a Rnd 3 of charts A and B. Work Calf Shaping chart from BOR (orange line at center), chart A 2 times, chart B 2 times, then Calf Shaping chart to BOR. Total 78 sts.

CUFF

Finish socks with cuff of your choice; see page 180 for options. Cuffs shown are 4-st cord BO.

FINISHING

Sew in yarn tails on WS, snugging up last st of zip line with tail hanging there.

> " Trust your own instinct. Your mistakes might as well be your own instead of someone else's.
>
> Billy Wilder
> ,,

Chart Layout

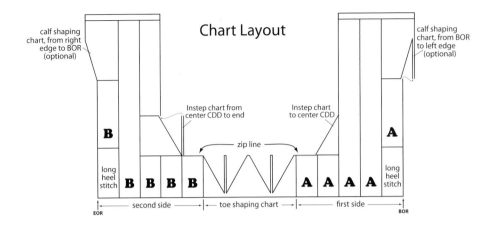

calf shaping chart, from right edge to BOR (optional)

calf shaping chart, from BOR to left edge (optional)

Instep chart from center CDD to end

Instep chart to center CDD

B

A

long heel stitch

B **B** **B** **B**

zip line

A **A** **A** **A**

long heel stitch

second side

EOR

toe shaping chart

first side

BOR

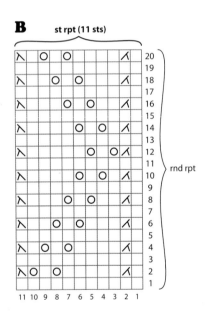

B st rpt (11 sts)

rnd rpt

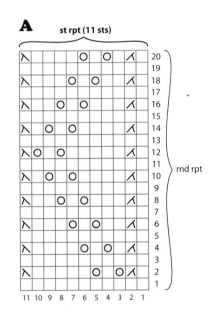

A st rpt (11 sts)

rnd rpt

☐ knit

○ YO

◺ k2tog

◹ ssk

⋏ CDD

∨ sl wyib

⊗ knit, wrapping twice

✳ see Zip Line in instructions

⧄ M1L

⧅ M1R

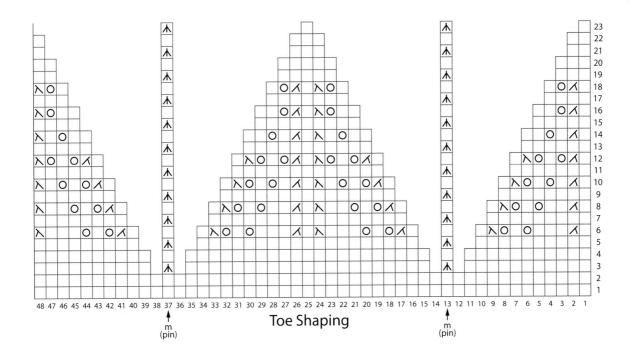

Toe Shaping

Long Heel Stitch

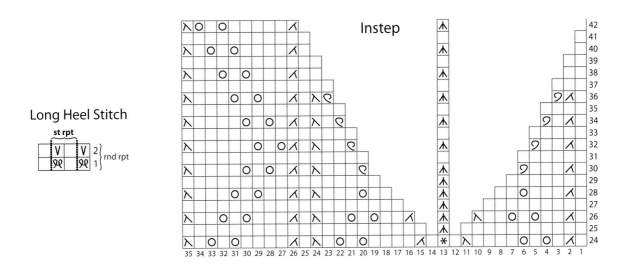

Instep

Calf Shaping

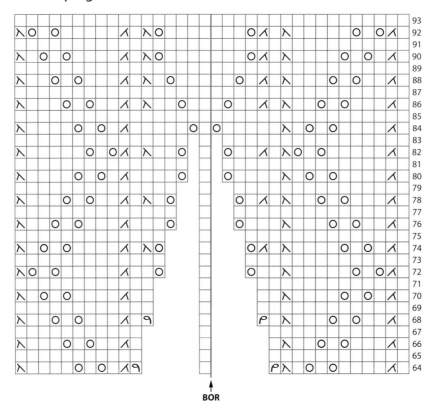

	knit		ssk
	YO		M1F
	k2tog		M1B

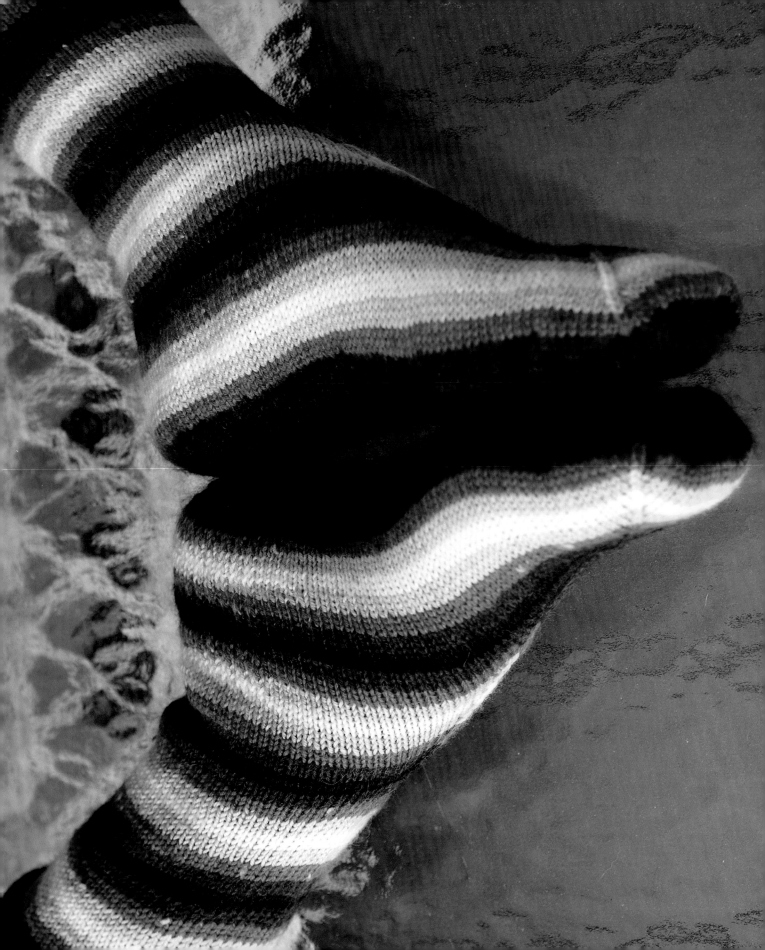

A Thicker Sole

Instructions below are for S (M, L) soles knitted at a gauge of 5 stitches and 7 rounds per inch. Do some swatches to find which yarn and needle combination will give you a nice firm sole fabric at that gauge. You might want a combination of yarns, such as two or three strands of fingering weight, or worsted weight plus reinforcement yarn.

A word to the wise: Check your gauge again about mid-way through the sole. If it's off a little, don't rip back and start over unless you really want to. As long as the firmness and thickness of the fabric is okay you can just add or subtract a round or two, increasing a few stitches around toe and heel if needed.

Holding selected yarns together and using a variation of JMCO (page 181), cast on 32 (35, 38) pairs of sts on 2 needle points. Total 64 (70, 76) sts.

Rnd 1 (set-up):
Needle 1: K1, M1F, k1, pm c1 for end of heel, k27 (30, 33), pm c2 for beginning of toe, k3. Needle 2: K1, M1L, k1, pm c2 for end of toe, k27 (30, 33), pm c3 for beginning of heel and BOR (3 sts remain on LN after BOR marker). There are 6 heel sts, 6 toe sts, and 27 (30, 33) sts on each side. Total 66 (72, 78) sts.

Rnd 2:
M1F, k6, M1F, sl m, k27 (30, 33), sl m, M1F, k6, M1F, sl m, k27 (30, 33), sl BOR m. Total 70 (76, 82) sts.

Odd numbered rnds 3 - 9:
Knit.

Rnd 4:
M1F, k2, M1F, (k1, M1F, k2, M1F) 2 times, sl m, k27 (30, 33), sl m, M1F, k2, M1F, (k1, M1F, k2, M1F) 2 times, sl m, k27 (30, 33), sl BOR m. Total 82 (88, 94) sts.

Rnd 6:
(M1F, k3) 2 times, M1F, k2, (M1F, k3) 2 times, M1F, k27 (30, 33). Do SRs around toe as follows: M1F, k4, M1F, k1, M1F, k4, M1F, k1, M1F, k4, M1F, k 8, w&t, p 36, w&t, k14, M1F, k1, M1F, k6, M1F, k1, M1F, k33 (36, 39), sl BOR m. Total 98 (104, 110) sts.

Rnd 8:
(k4, M1F) 4 times, k38 (41, 44), M1F, k1, M1F, k8, M1F, k1, M1F, k34 (37, 40), sl BOR m. Total 106 (112, 118) sts.

For size S, remove markers while working round 9 and end as follows: K12 to center heel. Total 106 sts. Cut yarn(s) that won't be used for sock top.

Rnd 10, sizes (M, L) only:
M1F, k5, M1F, k4, M1F, k6, M1F, k4, M1F, k5, M1F, k (30, 33), M1F, k8, (M1F, k4) 3 times, M1F, k8, M1F, k (30, 33), sl BOR m. Total (124, 130) sts.

For **size M**, remove markers while working round 10 and end as follows: K15 to center heel. Total 124 sts. Cut yarn(s) that won't be used for sock top.

Rnd 11, size L only:
Knit, removing markers, and end as follows: K15 to center heel. Total 130 sts. Cut yarn(s) that won't be used for sock top.

At this larger-than-usual gauge, the sole will be more comfortable if the smooth (knit) side is against your foot. To do this, just turn the knitting as if you were going to work flat (wrap before turning if using one of the sole yarns for the sock top). That is the only time you turn; the rest of the sock top will be done in the round, right side (public side) out as usual.

On the first round of the sock top, increase the stitch count to the number needed for your size. Distribute the increases evenly around the sides and toe, with none around the heel. The back of the heel and ankle will fit better that way.

OTHER OPTIONS FOR A THICKER SOLE

- Knit two soles separately with regular sock yarn following the sock pattern. Stop each sole having worked the second-to-last round, but cut the working yarn on only one. Place the two soles purl sides together (still on their own separate needles) and, using the working yarn still attached, join them on their last round by knitting together a stitch from each needle with a third needle. Then go on with the sock top, single thickness as usual.
- Double knitting — haven't tried it myself yet, but it would be an elegant way to accomplish a double-thick sole. On the last round, you would k2tog all around, to set up for a single-thickness sock top.

Techniques and Abbreviations

BO	Bind Off
BOR	Beginning of Round
c	color
Calf expansion options	*For a little expansion:* Change to the next larger needle size and work on in pattern without increases. The looser gauge won't affect durability of the sock because the leg doesn't get the hard wear that the foot does. *For more expansion:* Follow instructions in the pattern under "Calf Expansion by st increases." *For even more expansion:* Use both options above.
CC	Contrast Color
CDD(s)	**Centered Double Decrease(s):** slip 2 stitches together as if to knit 2 together, slip 1 purlwise, insert lefthand needle through front legs of the 3 stitches on righthand needle, knit 3 together.
CDD tbl	**Centered Double Decrease through back leg:** slip 1 purlwise, slip 1 through back leg purlwise, return both to lefthand needle, then do the centered double decrease as usual.
CDD that spans needle intersection	**Reposition all three stitches to lefthand needle, as follows:** *For double pointed needles or two circulars:* Slip the needed 1 or 2 stitches to the next lefthand needle without turning them, then do the centered double decrease as usual. *For one long circular needle (magic loop):* Stop before the first stitch needed for the CDD and pull lefthand needle cable through. Move the needle points into their usual working position and do the centered double decrease as usual.
cm	centimeter(s)
cn	cable needle
CO	Cast On

Cuff options

4-stitch cord BO (bind-off):

On RN, CO 4 sts (use your favorite provisional CO if you want to graft beginning of cord to end later). Without turning work or knitting the CO sts, sl 1 knitwise from LN to RN, insert LN into front legs of first 2 sts on RN (sock st and last CO st) and k2tog tbl. *Slip 4 sts from RN to LN, k3, ssk (using last cord st and next sock st). Repeat from * around until cord is joined to all sock sts. If you did not use a provisional CO, bind off the 4 sts, cut yarn leaving an 8" tail, and sew BO to CO. If you used a provisional CO, cut yarn leaving a 10" tail, and graft the 4 live sts to the provisional CO sts.

5-stitch knit & purl cord BO (bind-off):

On RN, CO 5 sts (use your favorite provisional CO if you want to graft beginning of cord to end later). Without turning work or knitting the CO sts, bring yarn to front, sl 1 from LN to RN, insert LN into back legs of first 2 sts on RN (sock st and last CO st) and p2tog. *Slip 5 sts from RN to LN, k1, k1 tbl, p1, k1 tbl, p2tog (using last cord st and next sock st). Repeat from * around until cord is joined to all sock sts. If you did not use a provisional CO, bind off the 5 sts, cut yarn leaving an 8" tail, and sew BO to CO. If you used a provisional CO, cut yarn leaving a 10" tail, and graft the 5 live sts to the provisional CO sts.

facing with picot edge:

Rnds 1 - 6: Knit.
Rnd 7: *YO, k2tog, repeat from * to end of rnd.
Rnd 8: Knit.
Rnd 9: decrease stitch count by 10% as follows: divide sts by 10, *knit 2 less than that number, k2tog, repeat from * as many times as will fit in the rnd, k to end of rnd.
Rnds 10 - 12: Knit.
Bind off loosely, sew facing down loosely on WS.

half-twisted ribbing:

Rnd 1: *k1 tbl, p1, repeat from * to end of rnd.
Rnd 2: *k1, p1, repeat from * to end of rnd.
Repeat Rnds 1-2 to length desired, bind off loosely.

reverse linen stitch:

Rnd 1: *sl 1 wyib, p1, repeat from * to end of rnd.
Rnd 2: *p1, sl 1 wyib, repeat from * to end of rnd.
Repeat Rnds 1-2 to length desired, bind off loosely.

seed stitch:

Rnd 1: *k1, p1, repeat from * to end of rnd.
Rnd 2: *p1, k1, repeat from * to end of rnd.
Repeat Rnds 1-2 to length desired, bind off loosely.

dpn(s)   double pointed needle(s)

EOR   End of Round

ER	Every Round
g	gram(s)
Grafting (Kitchener stitch)	Orient the needles so that RN (righthand needle) is behind and parallel to LN (lefthand needle). Work as follows with yarn-threaded tapestry needle: 1. On back needle, go through first stitch as if to knit, leave stitch on needle. 2. On front needle, go through first stitch as if to purl, leave stitch on needle. 3. On back needle, go through first stitch as if to purl, pull it off needle. 4. On back needle, go through next stitch as if to knit, leave stitch on needle. 5. On front needle, go through first stitch as if to knit, pull it off needle. 6. On front needle, go through next stitch as if to purl, leave stitch on needle. Repeat steps 3 - 6, making the tension of the graft match that of the knitting.
"	inch(es)
JMCO	Judy's Magic Cast-On with bottom-needle-first variation: 1. Hold two needle points in right hand, one above the other, ends pointing left. 2. Let about 24 inches [61 cm] of the yarn tail hang down over bottom needle, end behind needle and ball (working yarn) in front. This is the first stitch on bottom needle. 3. On left hand, arrange tail over index finger, working yarn over thumb, with other three fingers holding both strands. 4. Pivot both needle points downward, move top needle point down behind and around strand coming from thumb, catching strand on needle. This is first stitch on top needle. 5. Pivot both needle points upward, move bottom needle point down behind and around strand coming from index finger, catching strand on needle. 6. Pivot both needle points downward, move top needle point down behind and around strand coming from thumb, catching strand on needle. Repeat steps 5 — 6. After last stitch (which is on top needle), rotate needles so the ends point to right. Drop both strands of yarn. Tail will be to left of working yarn; bring it in front of working yarn, around to the right, and hold it against top needle to keep it out of the way. Slide stitches on bottom needle to cable, pick up working yarn, and proceed with Round 1 (set-up). (See page 186 for an Internet tutorial on this technique.)
JSSBO	Jeny's Surprisingly Stretchy Bind Off Work the first stitch, knitting or purling as it presents. If the next stitch is knit, do a yarn-over from behind the righthand needle over it to the front, knit the stitch, then pass both the yarn-over and the stitch before it over the stitch just worked. If the next stitch is purl, do a yarn-over from in front of the righthand needle over it to the back, purl the stitch, then pass both the yarn-over and the stitch before it over the stitch just worked. Work to end of round. (See page 186 for an Internet tutorial on this technique.)
k	knit

knitwise	as if to knit
ktbl	knit through back leg
ktfl	knit through front leg
k2tog	knit 2 stitches together
k3tog	knit 3 stitches together
LC ktbl over ktbl	Left Cross, knit through back leg over knit through back leg: 1. Put working yarn to back. 2. Insert righthand needle purlwise from behind needle into front leg of second stitch on lefthand needle. 3. Pull first and second stitches off lefthand needle, letting first stitch drop to front. 4. Pick up dropped stitch from front with lefthand needle, without turning it. 5. Insert lefthand needle purlwise into front leg of first stitch on righthand needle, knit it through back leg. 6. Knit through back leg of first stitch on lefthand needle.
LC ktbl over p	Left Cross, knit through back leg over purl: 1. Put working yarn to front. 2. Insert righthand needle purlwise from behind needle into front leg of second stitch on lefthand needle. 3. Pull first and second stitches off lefthand needle, letting first stitch drop to front. 4. Pick up dropped stitch from front with lefthand needle, without turning it. 5. Insert lefthand needle knitwise into back leg of first stitch on righthand needle, purl. 6. Knit through back leg of first stitch on lefthand needle.
LN	Lefthand Needle
Long Heel Stitch	*Rnd 1:* *k1, k1 wrapping twice, rpt from *. *Rnd 2:* *k1, slip 1 letting extra wrap fall, rpt from *. Repeat rnds 1-2 to length desired.
m	marker
M1B	Make 1 Back: Make loop around finger from back to front, twist loop ¼ turn to the left and put it on righthand needle.
M1F	Make 1 front: Make loop around finger from front to back, twist loop ¾ turn to the right and put it on righthand needle. Note that the resulting loop is oriented with its righthand leg at the back of the needle. You must, therefore, work into the back leg of this loop on the following round.

M1L	Make 1 Left: Insert lefthand needle under strand between stitches from front to back and knit into back leg.
M1LO	Make 1 Lift Only: Insert lefthand needle under strand between stitches from front to back and knit into front leg. This makes a little hole on purpose.
M1R	Make 1 Right: Insert lefthand needle under strand between stitches from back to front and knit into front leg.
MC	Main Color
mm	millimeter(s)
NA	Not Applicable
oz	ounce(s)
pm	place marker
p	purl
p2tog	purl 2 together
purlwise	as if to purl
psso	pass slipped stitch over
RC ktbl over ktbl	Right Cross, knit through back leg over knit through back leg: 1. Put working yarn to back. 2. Slip two stitches purlwise from lefthand needle to righthand needle. 3. Insert lefthand needle knitwise from behind needle into back leg of second stitch on righthand needle. 4. Pull righthand needle out of first and second stitches, letting first stitch drop to front. 5. Pick up dropped stitch from front with righthand needle, without turning it. 6. Insert lefthand needle purlwise into front leg of first stitch on righthand needle, knit it through back leg. 7. Knit through back leg of first stitch on lefthand needle.
RC ktbl over p	Right Cross, knit through back leg over purl: 1. Put working yarn to back. 2. Slip two stitches purlwise from lefthand needle to righthand needle. 3. Insert lefthand needle knitwise from behind needle into back leg of second stitch on righthand needle. 4. Pull righthand needle out of first and second stitches, letting first stitch drop to front.

5. Pick up dropped stitch from front with righthand needle, without turning it.

6. Insert lefthand needle purlwise into front leg of first stitch on righthand needle, knit it through back leg.

7. Purl first stitch on lefthand needle.

RN	Righthand Needle
rnd(s)	round(s)
rpt	repeat
RS	Right Side, also known as outside or public side
Sk2togP	Slip, knit 2 together, Pass: Slip 1 knitwise, knit 2 together, pass slipped stitch over.
sl	slip purlwise with yarn in back, unless otherwise instructed
SR(s)	Short Rows: 1. Knit the designated number of stitches. 2. Wrap next stitch as follows: slip it to righthand needle, pass working yarn to front between needles, slip stitch from righthand needle back to lefthand needle. 3. Turn work, pass working yarn to front between needles, purl the designated number of stitches. 4. Wrap next stitch as follows: slip it to righthand needle, pass working yarn to back between needles, slip stitch from righthand needle back to lefthand needle. 5. Turn work, pass working yarn to back between needles, continue round as usual. When you come to the wrapped stitches, hide the wraps by working them with the stitch they wrap.
ssk	slip, slip, knit: Slip 2 stitches one at a time knitwise, insert lefthand needle into front legs of first 2 stitches on righthand needle, knit 2 together.
sskSPS	slip, slip, knit, Slip, Pass, Slip: 1. Slip 2 stitches one at a time knitwise, insert lefthand needle into front legs of first 2 stitches on righthand needle, knit 2 together. 2. Slip stitch just made back to lefthand needle, pass next stitch over it. 3. Slip stitch back to righthand needle.
sssk	slip, slip, slip, knit: Slip 3 stitches one at a time knitwise, insert lefthand needle into front legs of first 3 stitches on righthand needle, knit 3 together.
st(s)	stitch(es)
tbl	through back leg

tfl   through front leg

w&t   wrap and turn:
Slip 1 purlwise, bring yarn between needles to opposite side, return slipped stitch
to lefthand needle, turn the work, put yarn in working position (in front or back of
needles as needed for next stitch).

WS   Wrong Side, also known as inside or non-public side

YO   Yarn-Over

yd(s)   yard(s)

zip line   A line of consecutive centered double decreases which join two areas of live stitches. It
is worked as follows:
1. Slip 1 stitch from righthand needle to lefthand needle.
2. Do a centered double decrease.
3. Slip the stitch just made back to lefthand needle.
Work these three steps as many times as specified in instructions.

Resources

YARNS

Some of the lovely yarns used for socks in this book were provided by these generous companies; visit their websites to see more of their excellent yarns:

Skacel Collections
www.skacelknitting.com

Blue Moon Fiber Arts
www.bluemoonfiberarts.com

INTERNET

JMCO (Judy's Magic Cast-On) as it is used in this book:
http://curiousknitter.blogspot.com/2011/02/judys-magic-cast-on-la-jeny.html

JSSBO (Jeny's Surprisingly Stretchy Bind Off):
http://www.youtube.com/watch?v=abBhe-JYmgI

If you find it hard to believe that charts can bend, check out JC Briar's Stitch Maps:
Stitch-Maps.com

Gratitude

I am deeply grateful to these fine people in my virtual village:

Cat Bordhi and the Visionary Authors
Ralph Waldo Emerson said "Do not follow where the path may lead. Go, instead, where there is no path and leave a trail." For decades, my knitting has taken me where there was no path. Now, thanks to Cat and the Visionaries, I have finally been able to leave a trail.

Deborah Robson for expert editorial advice and consistently generous sharing of her vast knowledge of all things publishing-related

Zoë Lonergan for bringing my vision into beautiful being on the printed page

Barbara Benson for taking on this photographic challenge in a cheerful, creative, energetic, and totally committed way

models: Jennifer Gibson, Fatimah Hinds, Karen L. Hines, Michele Owen, Jamie Collins, and Tiffany Roan — thank you, ladies, for your fortitude, unfailing patience, and heroic foot levitation

JC Briar for reliable clear-headedness and so much solidly helpful consultation

Jamie McCanless for meticulous tech editing and for being a thoroughly admirable human being

Nancy Marchant for getting me over the Illustrator hump

Cookie A for her ingenious and inspirational depiction of chart layout in *knit. sock. love.*

Jeane deCoster for much-appreciated encouragement to be true to my nerdy, super-analytical self

Burtch Hunter for kindly providing production advice

Charlotte Quiggle for generous suggestions about pattern format

Brenda Dayne for coming up with just the right press name

test knitters: Sandy Crabtree, Judith Coats-Crowson, and Jeny Staiman for valuable feedback on the early designs

my family for moral support and patient tolerance of my lengthy distraction